Fashion Buckles

Common to Classic

Gerald H. McGrath
Janet Meana

Schiffer Publishing Ltd

77 Lower Valley Road, Atglen, PA 19310

Man in the moon, modern.

Printed in Hong Kong
ISBN: 0-7643-0215-9

Book design by Ian Robertson

We are interested in hearing from authors with book
ideas on related topics.

Back Cover: Author's photos by Kathleen Lord.

Published by Schiffer Publishing Ltd.
77 Lower Valley Road
Atglen, PA 19310
Phone: (610) 593-1777
FAX: (610) 593-2002
Please write for a free catalog.
This book may be purchased from the publisher.
Please include $2.95 for shipping.
Try your bookstore first.

Contents

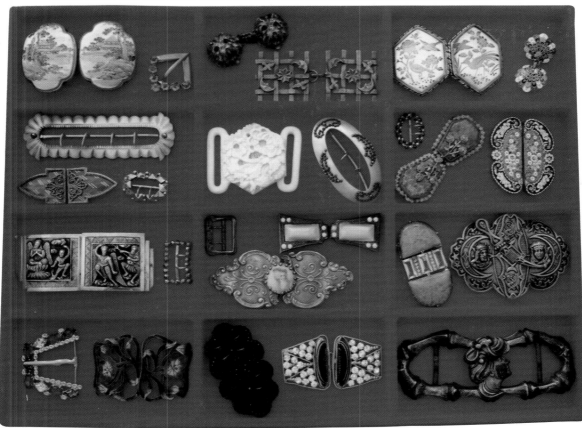

Display and storage tray. Such trays can be purchased for a minimal cost at flea markets, hobby shops, and craft stores. They are available in various sizes and colors and have a glass dust cover. A sensible way to store and protect collectibles.

Acknowledgments

The authors acknowledge with thanks the help received from the following: Joyce McGrath for her unending patience and her constant source of support, Irma Vadja for sharing her vast experience and knowledge, Clare Hatten for her aid and encouragement, and Janet Abbaduska for her research. We would also like to thank those who donated buckles to be photographed. Their names are included in the captions of their buckles.

Brass buckle with single prong closure.

Introduction

Mention buckles and most people think of the modern one-piece belt buckle consisting of a frame and a movable pin. Talk of collecting buckles and many think of men's buckles decorated with outdoor scenes, western themes, cigarette and beer logos, or military buckles.

The buckles we are writing of are from another world— a world of beauty, of handcrafted art, and of fashion. They are full of color and sparkle and come in various shapes and sizes that follow fashion trends as well as manufacturing techniques. The buckles in this book are primarily women's buckles and can be both decorative and functional. They are not museum pieces or made of costly crown jewels, but rather buckles that were produced for the middle class, some for everyday wear and others for dress-up occasions. They were used on belts, sashes, hats, shoes, trousers and capes.

There are several types of buckles, such as, slide, prong, clasp and interlock. A buckle is a single piece, complete in itself, consisting of a frame and a movable pin, and a clasp is a type of buckle consisting of two pieces, usually symmetrical. One part has a hook that fits into a slot on the other piece.

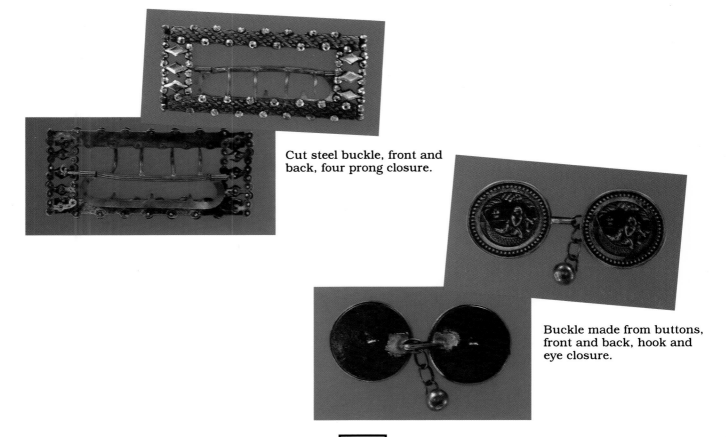

Cut steel buckle, front and back, four prong closure.

Buckle made from buttons, front and back, hook and eye closure.

Buckle, front and back, with metal loop closure.

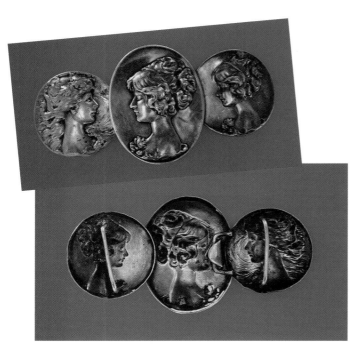

Clasp, front and back, two piece stamped metal, hook and eye closure.

The history of buckles is very closely associated with that of buttons, as are the materials with which they are made. While there have been many books devoted to button collecting, not much has been written about buckles. Bits and pieces of information can be found in jewelry, fashion and history books, as well as in some button books. Our book is an attempt to bring together as much information as we can on women's buckles. It is intended to be a buckle identification guide and not a technical reference.

Through history, pieces of jewelry, including buckles, have sometimes been altered or destroyed when they have gone out of style. We also hope to create an awareness of the beauty and craftsmanship found in old buckles so they are preserved for future generations.

The primary classification of buckles in this book is by material, which have been divided into four major categories; glass, metal, plastic and natural. Information on the individual materials can be found at the beginning of each chapter. Each photograph is individually captioned including information about the fastener type, any information that may be "marked" on the piece, the approximate date of manufacturing, a description including size, and a price range.

Prices in this book have been arrived at by extensive research and years of being involved in buckle collecting. Hallmarks and trademarks, which help identify when and where a piece was created, add value. Since information on hallmarks and trademarks can be found in books devoted to the subject, we have only included what is marked on the buckles for identification purposes. Buckles on their original cards or in their original boxes have an increased value. The condition of the buckle also influences its price. But the actual prices are determined by what someone is willing to pay for a particular buckle, which is a personal, subjective amount based on appreciation of beauty and craftsmanship. Buckles are beginning to be purchased as an investment, as well as for their beauty and uniqueness, which is forcing their prices up.

There are not many people who collect only buckles, most collections are a side line to button collections. Because they aren't looked at as collectibles on their own, they can still be found at flea markets, garage sales, antique shops, auctions, button shows and estate sales.

History of Buckles

Buckles have been around since ancient times. History and archeology books tell of buckles used to fit harnesses on animals and to hold weapons and garments in place for people. The popularity of buckles as adornments fluctuated according to fashion and politics. Archaeologists have discovered primitive belts with buckles dating back to the Bronze Age, circa 3500 to 1000 B.C., and in the Middle Ages, 476 A.D. to circa 1450 A.D., buckles were commonly used for capes, shoes and armor. These buckles were massive in size and studded with colored glass or jewels, or embossed with ornamental bronze.

In the seventeenth century, shoe and garter buckles became popular in Europe and America. In the late seventeenth century, in Birmingham, England, the craft of buckle making started and was firmly established by the beginning of the eighteenth century. In the early 1700s, knee buckles became fashionable for men's knee breeches and smaller buckles started appearing as purely decorative fashion accessories.

Up until the start of the Industrial Revolution in 1760, only the elite were able to enjoy fine jewelry and fashion accessories. The Industrial Revolution made buckles more accessible to the common people. With the new technology, fashion accessories became more affordable and were available in greater quantities.

In order to identify how and when a piece was made, it is necessary to study the historical sequence of events that was the Industrial Revolution. The following is a list of events that influenced fashion trends including buckles, beginning with the Late Georgian Period, early 19th Century. George III of Great Britain died in 1820, and George IV became king.

1819 Oxyhydrogen gas blowpipe was invented.
1824 Pinmaking machine patented in England by Lemuel Wellman Wright.
1830 India rubber elastic first appears in women's clothing.
1836 Edmund Davey discovers and identifies acetylene.

The EARLY VICTORIAN (ROMANTIC) PERIOD begins in 1837 when Victoria becomes Queen of Great Britain.

1837 The telegraph is patented.
1839 Charles Goodyear invents vulcanized rubber.
1840 Electroplating commercialized; large scale jewelry manufacturing begins in the United States.
circa 1840 Scottish motifs in agate jewelry popularized and continued to be so through the rest of century. Repoussé and machine stamping replace cannetille (gold filigree).
1842 Gutta-percha introduced in Paris.
1844 Goodyear patents vulcanized rubber,
1849 Gold electroplating patented.
1849 Opals first discovered in Australia.
1851 First international exhibition, the Great Exhibition of the Works of Industry of All Nations, held at the Crystal Palace of London.
1851 Artificial aventurine (goldstone) exhibited at the Crystal Palace.
1851 Goodyear displays products at Crystal Palace.
1853 Crystal Palace Exhibition held in New York, modeled after London exhibition.
1855 Theodor Fahrner established jewelry factory in Pforzheim, Germany.
circa 1855 First aluminum jewelry made in France.
1855 Paris Exposition Universelle is held and aluminum articles are first exhibited.
1855 R.W. Bunsen develops gas-air burner.
1857 Furnace to melt platinum and its alloys developed in Paris by Henri Ste. Claire Deville.
1857 Snake-chain making machine patented in United States.

MID VICTORIAN (GRAND) PERIOD

1861 Prince Consort Albert dies and Victoria enters prolonged period of mourning.
1861 to circa 1880 The wearing of mourning (black) jewelry required at British court.

circa 1862 Couturier Paul Poiret opens Boutique Chichi and introduces corsetless dresses and the vertical line in fashion.

1862 International Exhibition held in London at which Archaeological Revival gold jewelry was exhibited by Castellani of Rome.

1867 Paris Exposition is held at which Egyptian revival jewelry was exhibited.

1869 Gorham Mfg. Co. of Providence, Rhode Island, adopts sterling standard of 925 parts per thousand.

1869 Celluloid, the first successful semi synthetic thermoplastic, was invented in the U.S. by John Wesley Hyatt; commercial production begins in 1872; tradename registered in 1873.

1870s Influx of European craftsmen and designers into the U.S. and Japanese craftsmen introduced metal-working techniques and designs to the West.

1872 International Exhibition held in London.

1873 Universal Exhibition held in Vienna.

1873 U.S. establishes gold standard.

1875 The Celluloid Novelty Co. begins jewelry production.

1876 Centennial Exhibition held in Philadelphia.

1877 Advent of bottled oxygen, liquefied and compressed.

1877 B. Blumenthal & Co., Inc. established in New York City, maker of buttons and buckles.

1878 Paris Exhibition Universelle is held.

LATE VICTORIAN (AESTHETIC) PERIOD

1887 Queen Victoria's Golden Jubilee is celebrated.

1888 C.R. Ashbee's Guild of Handicraft established in London, the first guild to specialize in jewelry making and metalwork.

1889 Paris Exhibition Universelle is held, the Eiffel Tower is constructed which is the first structure to serve as a landmark for an exhibition.

1891 The enactment of the McKinley Tariff Act requires that foreign imports be marked, in English, with the name of the country of origin.

1891 Power-driven bruting or girdling machine was patented for cutting diamonds and improved production of old European cut, round brilliant diamonds.

1893 World's Columbian Exhibition is held in Chicago.

1893 Cultured pearls first developed by Mikimoto in Japan; first spherical pearls grown in 1905.

1895 Samuel Bing opens his new Paris gallery of decorative art called L'Art Nouveau.

1895 René Lalique exhibits jewelry at the Bing gallery and the Salon of the Societé des Artistes Francais. He began work on a series of 145 pieces for Calouste Gulbenkian.

1895 Daniel Swarovski opens glass stone-cutting factory in Tyrol, Austria.

1897 Queen Victoria's Diamond Jubilee is celebrated.

1897 Casein plastics marketed in Germany.

1899 Fred Harvey Company provides Native American silversmiths with sheet silver and precut turquoise to produce first Indian-made tourist jewelry for Harvey House curio shops.

1900 Paris Exhibition Universelle is held.

1900 Oxyacetylene torch is invented by Edmund Fouché.

1900 Synthetic rubies exhibited at Paris Exhibition.

EDWARDIAN PERIOD (BELLE ÉPOQUE)

1901 Queen Victoria dies and Edward Vll becomes king. He is coronated in 1902.

1901 Pan American Exposition held in Buffalo, New York.

1901 Gustav Stickley begins publishing his periodical The Craftsman, until 1916.

1902 Vienna Secession Exhibition is held.

1904 Louisiana Purchase Exhibition held in St. Louis.

1904 Georg Jensen opens his silversmithy in Copenhagen, Denmark.

1905 Forest Craft Guild founded by Forest Mann in Grand Rapids, Michigan.

1906 National Stamping Act passed in U.S. requiring marking of gold and silver content.

1907 Leo Baekeland patents Bakelite, the first entirely synthesized plastic.

1908 First spherical pearls patented in Japan by Mikimoto. The American patent was granted in 1916.

1910 Edward the Vll dies.

circa 1910-1920 Suffragette jewelry in green, white, and violet (first initials for "give women votes") was popular.

1914 World War I began.

1914 Platinum is banned for use in jewelry during wartime.

1914 The first United States fashion show was held, by Edna Woolman Chase, the editor of Vogue.

1915 Panama-Pacific International Exposition held in San Francisco.
1918 World War I ended.
1918 Bohemia, Moravia and Slovakia became the Republic of Czechoslovakia.

THE MODERN ERA

1919 The Eighteenth Amendment to the United States Constitution is ratified, starting the era of prohibition.
1920 The Nineteenth Amendment to the United States Constitution is ratified, giving women the right to vote.
1922 Howard Carter discovered King Tutankhamun's tomb in Egypt.
1925 Exposition Internationale des Arts Decoratifs et Industriels Modernes held in Paris.
circa 1925 Synthetic spinel, inadvertently produced by flame fusion process 1908, was in wide commercial use.
1926 Motion pictures with sound was first publicly shown.
1926 The first commercial injection molding machine was patented by Eckert and Ziegler in Germany.
1927 Cartier presents model with spring system for double clip brooch.
1929 L'Exposition de Joaillerie et Orfévrerie, Precious Jewelry and Goldwork, is held in Paris.
1930 Formation of the Union des Artistes Modernes in Paris.
1931 William Spratling opens the first silver workshop in Taxco, Mexico.
1932 14k gold replaces 12k and 15k in Britain by decision of the Worshipful Company of Goldsmiths in London.
1933 Prohibition repealed.
1933 Gold taken out of circulation.
1934 Cecil B. De Mille's Cleopatra starring Claudette Colbert in the title role.
1935 D. Lisner & Co. introduces Bois Glacé jewelry, their trade name for colorless phenolic plastic (Bakelite) laminated to wood.
1937 Du Pont de Nemours & Co. introduces acrylic plastic, trade name Lucite.

1937 The International Exhibition of Arts and Techniques in Modern Life held in Paris.
1938 Du Pont develops nylon, the first all-synthetic fiber.
1939 The New York World's fair, entitled "The World of Tomorrow," opens.
1939 World War II begins in Europe.
1940 France falls under German occupation and the Bank of France bans all gold trading.
1941 Craft Horizons, the first national magazine for crafts, is published by the Handcraft League.
1942 Use of platinum for jewelry prohibited in the United States. White metal restricted by the United States government, sterling silver was used as substitute in costume jewelry.
1944 Ten percent luxury tax on jewelry in United States, raised to 20 percent.
1945 World War II ends.
circa 1945 Mexican government requires making of sterling silver with spread eagle assay mark.
1946 First national exhibit of American studio artists' jewelry held at Museum of Modern Art in New York City.
1954 First successful production of synthetic diamonds at General Electric; process patented in 1960; large gem-quality crystals produced in 1970.
1955 Swarovski Corp. introduces the Aurora Borealis color effect for rhinestones and crystal in collaboration with Christian Dior.
1961 International Exhibition of Modern Jewelry (1890-1961) held in London.
1961 United States National Stamping Act amended, requiring a maker's trademark.
1963 United States Post Office introduces the ZIP code.
1980 The original buckle collectors magazine "Basically Buckles," was established in LaMoure North Dakota.
1986 B. Blumenthal Co. purchased the Lansing Button Co. of Lansing, Iowa.
1994 B. Blumenthal Co. consolidated with the Lansing Co. and moved all its packaging and distribution to the Lansing, Iowa location.

Chapter One
Buckles Made From Glass

An area in the heart of Europe, known as Bohemia, is associated with glass-making. Several of the buckles we have photographed are marked with some form of the name "Czechoslovakia," which is part of Bohemia.

Glass has been made since ancient times and can be blown, blown-molded, pressed and tooled. Glass is often used as imitation gems and comes in several forms including canes, beads, rods and spun threads. Glass stones can be mounted in several ways including prong set, bezel set and pavé set or glued. Early glass stones, which were handmade and hand-polished, were called *mine cut* and lacked sharp facets. As time went by and the Industrial Revolution gained momentum, glass evolved into highly polished faceted stones. Machine made stones came to be known as *rhinestones*.

Rhinestones

In the early part of the twentieth century, a few tourist shops along the banks of the Rhine river in Germany sold jewelry with stones called *Rheinkiessel*. These stones were water clear and cut like diamonds and contained red, green and blue blotches. They were made from glass that was molded and cut in Bohemia and the red, green and blue patches had been ingeniously fused into the glass during the molding process. *Rheinkiesel,* literally translated, means Rhine pebbles. At some point, the small imitation diamonds were named rhinestones.

The addition of minerals to the glass achieved colors of blue, yellow, amber, red, purple, amethyst, black and opaque white. It has been said that in making transparent glass, man imitated natural rock crystal. In making colored glass, man imitated nature's precious and semi-precious stones.

Colored Glass

The natural color of glass is green which is caused by the metallic oxides and alkali mix from which glass is formed. Clear glass is achieved by adding glass makers soap. This ingredient, oxide of manganese, clears and washes out the color imparted by the other metallic oxides in the mixture. As knowledge was gained, other ingredients were added to control the color of green and to create new colors. An unlimited assortment of colors became available to coordinate with clothing.

Black Glass

When Queen Victoria went into mourning after her husband Albert died in 1861, black became the fashion color. Glass makers created jewelry which was called "jet" because of its color rather than the material from which it was made. True jet is a gem from a mineral found in bituminous shales and is rare. Chemically, jet is closely related to coal. It has been used in Whiteby, England, since 650 AD, when it was carved into ornaments. Chunks of jet were washed in by the sea and collected by the natives of Whiteby. When that mysterious source ended, jet was mined from the surrounding land.

Black glass can have a dull or a shiny surface, with the dull black glass being associated with mourning. Different formulas for coloring produced varying degrees of the intensity of black. While a buckle may seem to be a deep black, holding it against a strong light may reveal amethyst, blue-green, smoky opaque, or slightly iridescent variations.

Clasp, unmarked, c. 1920. Teardrop
shaped brass filigree base with prong set
rhinestones, 3.5" x 1.25". $30-40.

Buckle, unmarked, c. 1930.
Apple and leaf stem shaped
rhinestone, prong set, clear and
red stones set in brass, 3" x
1.5". $30-40.

Three clasps, unmarked, c. 1930. *Left to right*: Clasp, oval
shaped, brass filigree base with prong set rhinestones and two
large amber colored rhinestones, 2.5" x 1". $25-35. Clasp,
rectangular shaped, silver painted brass base with prong set
rhinestones and two cabochons centered on each side, 1.24" x
.75". $10-15. Clasp, rectangular shaped, pot metal base with
pavé set rhinestones and amber colored cabochons, 3.25" x .75".
$20-25.

Clasp, unmarked, c. 1930. Star shaped pot
metal base with pavé set rhinestones, 2.5" x
2.75". $25-30.

Buckle, marked "Czechoslov," c.
1935. Round, pot metal base with
pavé set rhinestones and green
bezel set center stones, 2.5" dia.
$35-40.

Buckle, unmarked, c. 1930. Square gold leaf coated brass base with prong set rhinestones, 2.6" x 2.6". $30-40.

Two clasps, one buckle. *Left*: Clasp, heart shaped pattern, prong set rhinestones in a brass base with a silver wash, 2" x 1". $20-30. *Middle*: Buckle, unmarked, c. 1930. Rectangular, brass base with prong set rhinestones, 1.75" x .75". $10-15. *Right*: Clasp, marked "Czechoslovakia," c. 1930. Diamond shaped, brass filigree base with prong set rhinestones, 2" x 1.25". $15-25

Clasp, unmarked, front and back, c. 1920. Diamond shaped pattern, brass base with prong set rhinestones, 4" x 1.5". $30-40.

Buckle, unmarked, c. 1935. Square shaped, gold leaf coated, brass base with rose and green colored prong set stones, and an inner row of clear rhinestones, 2" x 1.75". $25-35.

Buckle, unmarked, c. 1925. Rectangle, gold leaf coated, brass base with prong set small and large rhinestones, 3.5 " x 2". $20-30.

Four buckles, unmarked, c. 1925. *Left to right:* Buckle, round gold leaf coated brass base with prong set rhinestones, .8" dia.. $5-10. Buckle, square gold leaf coated base with prong set rhinestones, 1" x 1". $5-10. Buckle, oval shaped gold leaf coated brass base with prong set green rhinestones, 1" x .75". $5-10. Buckle, rectangle brass filigree base with prong set rhinestones, 1.5" x .8". $5-10.

Buckle, unmarked, c. 1925. Teardrop shaped, brass base with rows of prong set rhinestones, 2.75" x 1.5". $30-40.

Clasp, unmarked, c. 1930. Oval shaped, brass filigree, painted silver with outer row of prong set rhinestones, and two large centered red prong set rhinestones, centered, 2.75" x 2". $25-35.

Buckle, unmarked, c. 1930. Oval shaped, brass base with prong set rhinestones, 2.25" x 1.75". $20-25.

Buckle, unmarked, c. 1935. Rectangular shaped, brass base with prong set clear and blue glass stones, 2" x 1.5". $20-25.

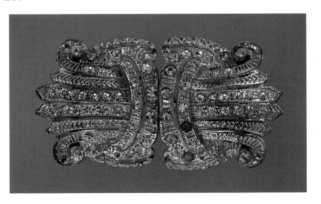

Clasp, unmarked, c. 1935. Crown shaped, white pot metal base with pavé set rhinestones, 2.75" x 1.50". $20-30.

Clasp, marked "made in Czechoslovakia," c. 1925. Crescent shaped ovals, brass base, painted silver with double row of prong set rhinestones and centered, triangle pattern of rhinestones, 2.75" x 1.50". $35-45.

Clasp, unmarked, c. 1935. Bow shaped, pot metal base with prong set rows of rhinestones, 3" x 2". $35-45.

Clasp, unmarked, c. 1940. Triangle shaped, pot metal base painted gold, bezel set rhinestones, 3.75" x 1.5". $20-30.

Buckle, unmarked, c. 1925. Oval shaped, with leaf of rhinestones, brass base with prong set rhinestones, 2.25" x 2". $25-30.

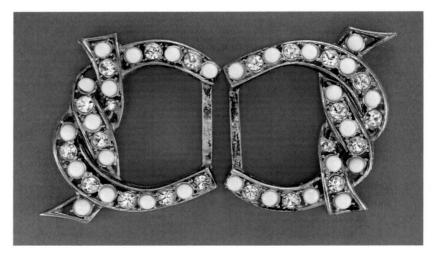

Buckle/slide, unmarked, c. 1940. Ribbon circles of pavé set rhinestones and white pearl beads in a white pot metal base, 3.75" x 2". $10-20.

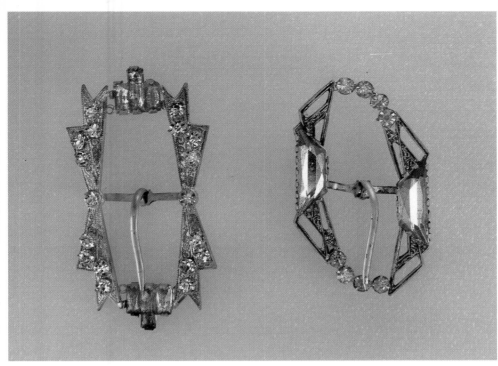

Buckle, unmarked, c. 1935. Square, plated pot metal with rows of pavé set rhinestones, 2" x 2". $15-25.

Buckles, unmarked, c. 1925. *Left*: Rectangular shaped, stamped brass base, silver painted with prong set rhinestones and baguettes, 3" x 2". $20-25. *Right*: Oblong shaped, stamped brass base, silver painted, brass base with prong set rhinestones and baguettes, 2.5" x 1.5". $20-25.

Two clasps, unmarked, c. 1925. *Left*: Shell shaped, silver painted brass filigree base with prong set rhinestones, 1.75" x .75". $10-15. *Left*: Six sided, brass filigree base with prong set rhinestones, 2.5" x 1.25". $20-25.

Buckles, unmarked, c. 1900. *Top*: Rectangle, silver painted brass base with prong set rhinestones, 4" x 1.25". $20-25. *Bottom*: Rectangle, brass base with prong set rhinestones, 7" x 1.75". $30-40.

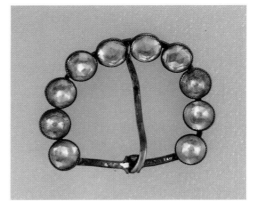

Buckle, unmarked, c. 1900. Half circle shaped, silver painted brass base with bezel set rhinestones, 2" x 1.5". $20-25.

Buckle, unmarked, c. 1935. Square shaped nickel plated brass base with prong set rhinestones, 1.25" x 1". $10-15.

Buckle, marked "solid bronze," with Patent #, c. 1960. Rectangle, bronze base with prong set stones on tang of buckle, 2.5" x 1.25". $5-10.

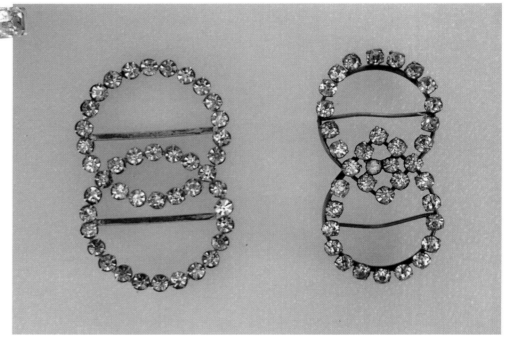

Buckle/slide, c. 1925. *Left*: Intertwined circles, brass base with prong set rhinestones, 2.5" x 1.5". $15-20. *Right:* Intertwined circles with diamond shaped center, marked "Czechoslovakia," brass base with prong set rhinestones, 2.5" x 1.5". $20-25.

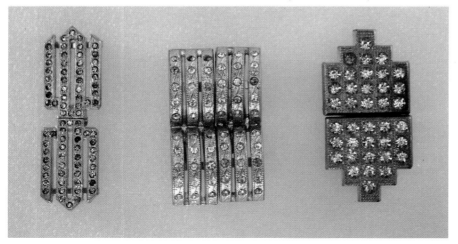

Clasps, unmarked, c. 1935. *Left*: Classic shaped white pot metal with pavé set rhinestones, 1.75" x 1". $5-15. *Middle*: Joined, half circle shaped, white pot metal with pavé set rhinestones, 1.75" x 1". $10-15. *Right*: Step shaped ends, white pot metal with pavé set rhinestones, 2" x .60". $5-10.

Clasp, unmarked, c. 1930. Classic shell design, silver painted brass base with prong set rhinestones, 2.25" x 1.5". $20-30.

Clasp, unmarked, c. 1930. Classic design, cast white pot metal with pavé set rhinestones, 2.75" x 1.25". $15-25.

Clasp, marked "Czechoslovakia," c. 1920. Teardrop shaped, brass filigree base with prong set rhinestones, 2.5" x 1". $30-40.

Buckles, c. 1930. *Left*: Unmarked, oval, brass base with prong set rhinestones, 2.5" x 1". $15-20. *Right*: Marked "Czechoslovakia," Circle, brass base with prong set rhinestones, 2" dia.. $20-25.

Clasp, unmarked, c. 1940. Diamond shaped, cast base of pot metal and pink Bakelite with pavé set rhinestones, 3.25" x 2". $15-25.

Clasp, marked "T&G", c. 1945. Teardrop shaped, cast white pot metal base with pavé set rhinestones, centers of orange Bakelite flowers, 4.5" x 1.5". $10-20

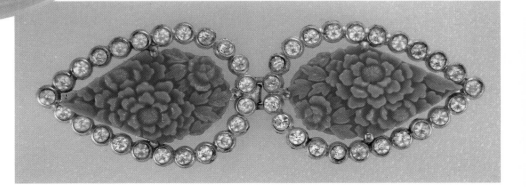

Clasp, unmarked, c. 1940. Circles of Bakelite and white pot metal with pavé set rhinestones, 5" x 1.25". $20-30.

Clasp, unmarked, c. 1930. *Left*: Rectangle shape, cast white pot metal base with pavé rhinestones, 2.5" x 1". $5-10. *Right*: Ribbon circles of cast white pot metal with pavé set rhinestones and baguettes, 2.25" x 1.5". $10-20.

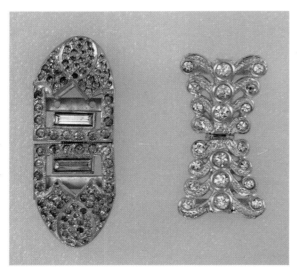

Clasp, unmarked, c. 1930. *Left*: Rectangle shaped ribbons of cast white pot metal and pavé set rhinestones, 1.75" x 1". $5-10. *Right*: Rectangle shaped, white pot metal base with pavé set rhinestones and baguettes, 2.25" x .75". $10-15.

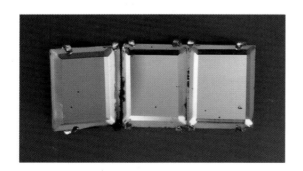

Clasp, marked "WMCA 19," c. 1935. Rectangle shaped, cast base of white pot metal with prong set mirrored glass, 2.5" x 1". $15-20.

Buckle, unmarked, c. 1900. Hat buckle, square shaped, stamped brass with double prong closure and prong set rhinestones, 4.75 "x 5.25". $50-75.

Clasp, unmarked, on card marked, "Jeweled Dress Buckle, "GOODY", Made in U.S.A.," c. 1935. Pavé set rhinestones, silver, on base metal, 2.25" x 1", card is 3.5" x 2.5". $10-15.

Buckle, unmarked, c. 1920. Oblong, brass base with two rows of prong set rhinestones, single closure, 4.5" x 1.5". $20-30.

Buckles, salesman's sample card marked, "CARD 212, Trade Mark Registered, Beaver Brand, Thru industry we thrive, Price per dozen," c. 1930. Partial card of pavé set rhinestone buckles, silver and gold, painted base metal. *Clare Hatten collection*.

Clasp, unmarked, c. 1930. Oval shape circles of white base metal with pavé set rhinestones, 3.5" x 1.25". $20-30.

Belt, marked, "WMCA," c. 1930. Rows of prong set rhinestones sewn to a satin base, cast, white metal clasp, 1" x 26". $75-100.

Sash buckle, unmarked, c. 1910. Oval shaped with prong set rhinestones, set in a brass base, 4.75" x 2.25". $30-40.

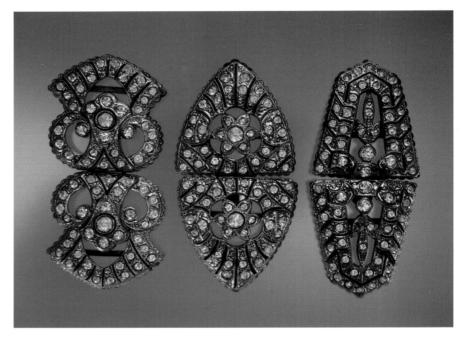

Three clasps, unmarked, c. 1930. *Left to Right*: Classic design, white base metal with pavé set rhinestones, 2.75" x 1.4". $20-30. Diamond shaped, white base metal with pavé set rhinestones, 2.8" x 1.4". $20-30. Rectangular shape, white base metal with pavé set rhinestones, 3" x 1.5". $20-30.

Buckle, unmarked, c. 1935. Diamond shape, gold washed brass base with prong set rhinestones, single prong closure, 2.25" x 2.25". $20-30.

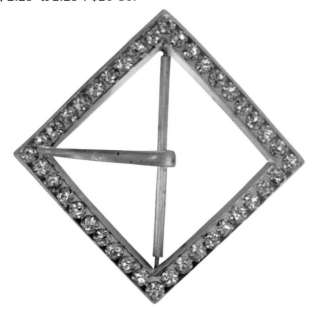

Buckle, unmarked, c. 1930. Oval design,double row of prong set rhinestones in a brass base with a single closure prong, 2.78" x 2.25". $20-30.

Buckles, unmarked, c. 1935. *Left*: Shamrock shaped, brass base with prong set rhinestones, single prong closure, 2" x 2.25". $10-15. *Right*: Rectangle brass base with prong set rhinestones, 1.5" x 1". $10-15.

Buckle, unmarked, c. 1925. Angled peaks of pavé set rhinestones set in a pot metal base, 2.25" x 1.25". $15-25.

Belt, unmarked, c. 1930. Rows of prong set rhinestones sewn to a padded satin cloth, rectangle shaped clasp with pavé set rhinestones and baguettes, .75" x 30". $75.

Clasps, unmarked, c. 1935. *Left*: Leaf shape, white base metal with pavé set rhinestones, 3" x 1". $15-20. *Right*: Angle shape, white base metal with pavé set rhinestones, 3.25" x 1.5". $15-20.

Buckles, unmarked, c. 1925. *Top*: Rectangle, brass base with prong set rhinestones, single closure prong, 3" x 2.25". $15-25. *Bottom*: Diamond shape, brass base with prong set rhinestones, single closure prong, 4" x 1". $15-25.

Clasp, unmarked, c. 1900. Oblong, brass filigree base with prong set rhinestones and bezeled foil under glass centers, 2.25" x 1". $35-50.

Buckle, unmarked, c. 1915. Diamond shape, brass base with prong set rhinestones, 4" x 2". $20-30.

Belt, unmarked, c. 1935. Shell shape oval clasp of prong set rhinestones, two bezel set blue faceted glass gems at the center fastened to a purple satin cloth, clasp is, 2.75" x 1.75", overall length, 40". $40-50.

Clasp, unmarked, c. 1930. Square shaped, white base metal, and metal mount for large amber colored stones, and pavé set rhinestones, 2.5" x 1.5". $25-35.

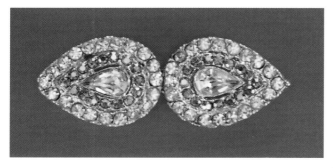

Clasp, unmarked, c. 1955. Teardrop shaped white base metal with pavé set rhinestones, 2.5" x 1". $5-10.

Clasp, marked "Czechoslovakia," c. 1920. Square brass filigree base with prong set rhinestones and large cut glass center stones, 1.75" x 1.25". $30-40.

Clasp, unmarked, c. 1900. Unusual design, rhinestones prong set in a brass rope base with large center stones, 3.5" x 1". $40-50.

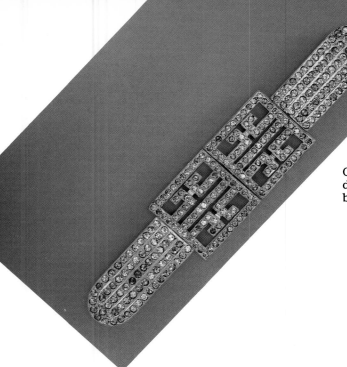

Clasp, unmarked, c. 1925. Rectangular, Greek design, rows of pavé set rhinestones in a cast base, 5.75" x 1.25". $30-40.

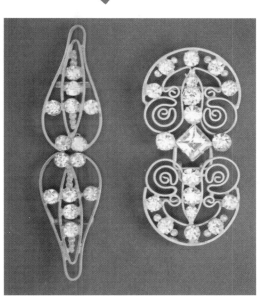

Two clasps, c. 1920. *Left*: Marked "Czechoslovakia," teardrop shape brass filigree base with prong set rhinestones, 3.25" x .75". $30-40. *Right*: Oval shaped brass filigree base with prong set rhinestones, 2.25" x 1.25". $25-35.

Buckle/Button set, unmarked, c. 1930. Square shaped plated base with individual bezel set rhinestones, single prong closure, buckle, 1.5" x 1.5", button, .375". $25-35.

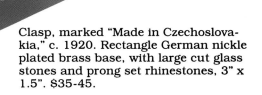

Clasp, marked "Made in Czechoslovakia," c. 1920. Rectangle German nickle plated brass base, with large cut glass stones and prong set rhinestones, 3" x 1.5". $35-45.

Clasp, marked "Made in Czechoslovakia," c. 1925. Diamond shaped German nickle plated brass base, with large prong set glass stones, 3" x 1.5". $35-45.

Buckle, unmarked, c. 1915. Six sided prong set rhinestones set in a brass base, with single prong closure, 2.75" x 2.5". $25-35.

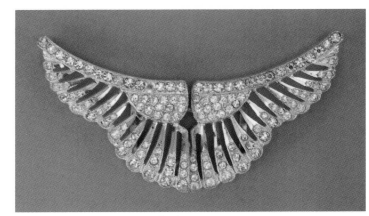

Clasp, unmarked, c. 1915. Full wing spread shape, cast white pot metal base with pavé set rhinestones, 3.75" x 2.25". $30-40.

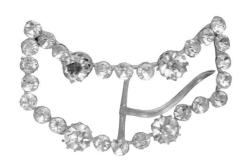

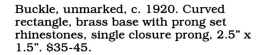

Buckle, unmarked, c. 1920. Curved rectangle, brass base with prong set rhinestones, single closure prong, 2.5" x 1.5". $35-45.

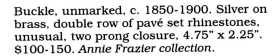

Buckle, unmarked, c. 1850-1900. Silver on brass, double row of pavé set rhinestones, unusual, two prong closure, 4.75" x 2.25". $100-150. *Annie Frazier collection.*

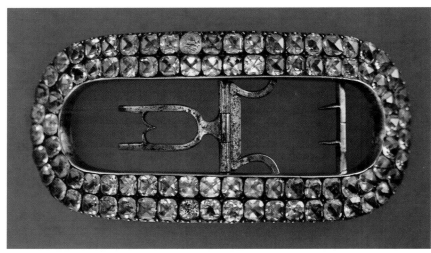

Two clasps, c. 1925. *Left*: Unmarked, teardrop shape, brass filigree base with circles of prong set rhinestones, 2.25" x 1". $20-25. *Right*: Marked "Made in Czecho Slovakia," heart shaped, with brass filigree base, with circles of prong set rhinestones, 2" x 1". $30-35.

Belt, unmarked, c. 1930. Silver on brass shell shaped, with a row of prong set rhinestones down the center, fastened to a green satin cloth. Clasp is 1.5" x 1". Overall length, 28". $50.

Clasp, front and back, marked "WMCA, Queen co.," c. 1935. White base metal with pavé set rhinestones and a large prong set topaz colored glass stone, 2.5" x 1.25". $25-35.

Clasp, marked "Made in Czechoslovakia," c. 1910. Step shaped, brass base with rows of prong set rhinestones, 3" x 1.25". $25-35.

Clasp, unmarked, c. 1935. Circles of pavé set rhinestones in a white metal base with a large faceted glass stone at center, 1.75" x .875. $20-25.

Clasp, unmarked, c. 1920. Two large peach colored glass stones surrounded by pavé set rhinestones in a base metal, 2" x 1". $35-50.

Clasp, unmarked, c. 1900. Butterfly shaped imitation cut steels, pressed black glass, wired to a brass base, 3" x 2.75". $40-50.

Clasp, unmarked, c. 1890. Pressed black glass butterfly design, mounted on a brass plate, 2" x 2.25". $40-50

Clasp, unmarked, c. 1890. Pressed black glass clover leaves, mounted on a brass plate, 2.75" x 1.5". $30-40.

Clasp, unmarked, c. 1890. Pressed black glass triangles with flowered pattern, mounted on brass plates, 2.5" x 2". Notice chipped corner. $20-30.

Clasp, unmarked, c. 1910. Pressed black glass, shield design, mounted on a brass plate, 2" x 2.5". $40-50.

Buckle, unmarked, c. 1890. Passementerie style, pressed black glass beads mounted on wire back and cloth, 2.5" x 1.25". $20-30.

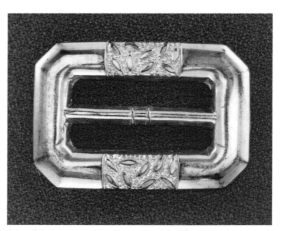

Buckle, unmarked, c. 1900. Rectangle, pressed black glass with gold luster finish, note missing closure prong, 2.5" x 1.75". $15-25.

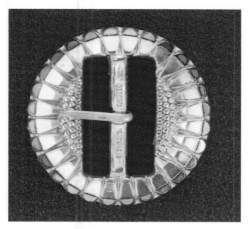

Buckle, marked "Czecho Slovakia,"c. 1900. Round pressed black glass, scalloped pattern with a gold luster finish, single prong closure, 2.25"dia.. $20-25.

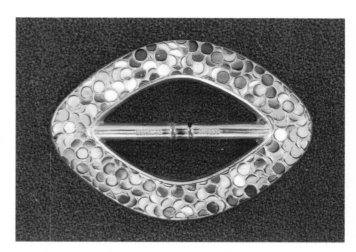

Buckle, marked "Czecho Slovakia," c. 1900. Oval shaped pressed black glass, scale pattern with gold luster finish, note missing closure prong, 3" x 2.25". $20-25.

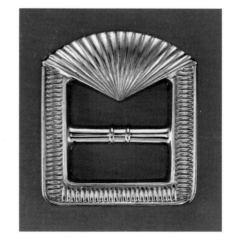

Buckle, marked "Made in Czecho Slovakia," c. 1900. Rectangle shape, black pressed glass with a silver luster, shell pattern on one end, note missing closure prong, 2.25" x 1.75". $20-25.

Clasp, marked "Czecho", c. 1910. Oblong pressed black glass with gold trim bordered by triangles of prong set rhinestones set in a brass rope base, 2.75" x 1.5". $60-70.

Clasp, unmarked,c. 1910. Faceted pressed black glass set in a brass base, trimmed with triangles of prong set rhinestones, 3.5" x 1.5". $50-75.

Buckle, unmarked, c. 1915. Half circle of pressed black glass stones, separated by prong set rhinestones in a brass base and a silver wash, 2.25" x 1.5". $20-25.

Buckle/hat pin set, unmarked, c. 1900. Bezel set pressed black glass, rounded, half circles, seperated by bezel set rhinestones in a brass base, single prong closure, 2" square, matching hat pin, single bezel set rhinestone, three fanned black glass stones, with a single fastener stone, 1.5" 3.5". $75-100.

Buckle, belt ornament, marked "E.F," c. 1900. Oval shaped, prong set rhinestones set in a brass filigree base with a large faceted black glass stone, bezel set, 3" x 2.5". $50-60.

Clasp, marked "R K," c. 1920. Circles of pressed black glass joined by pavé set rhinestones in pot metal, 4.5" x 2". $25-35.

Clasps, unmarked, c. 1915. *Top*: Geometric design of pressed black glass with brass mounts, 3" x 1.25". $20-30. *Bottom*: Rectangles with geometric arrow, with brass mounts, 2.25" x 1.25". $20-30.

Clasps, marked "Made in Czechoslovakia," c. 1915. *Top*: Angled cut, pressed black glass with brass mounts, 2" x 1.5". $20-30. *Bottom*:Angled cut, geometric design of pressed black glass with brass mounts, 2.5" x 1.25". $20-30.

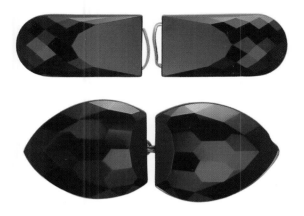

Clasps, marked "Made in Czcho Slovakia," c. 1915. *Top*: Rectangle shaped, geometric design, pressed black glass, 3" x .75". $20-30. *Bottom*: Geometric design, pressed black glass with brass mount, note chip on left corner, 3" x 1.25". $25-30.

Clasp, unmarked, c. 1910. Rectangular shaped pressed black glass, mounted in a brass base with filigree trim, 2.5" x 2". $30-40.

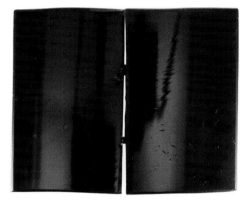

Clasp, unmarked, c. 1890. Pressed black rectangles, mounted on brass plates, 2.75" x 2.25". $30-40.

Clasp, unmarked, c. 1900. Pressed black glass with shell design and gold trim set in a brass base, 2.5" x 1". $25-30.

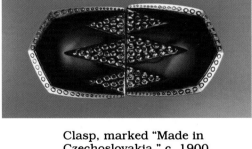

Clasp, marked "Made in Czechoslovakia," c. 1900. Pressed black glass with silver trim and brass catch and mounts, 2.5" x 1". $30-40.

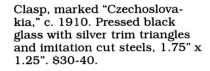

Clasp, marked "Czechoslova-kia," c. 1910. Pressed black glass with silver trim triangles and imitation cut steels, 1.75" x 1.25". $30-40.

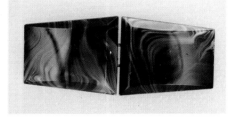

Clasp, marked "Czecho-slovakia," c. 1920. Six sided convexed geometric design of pressed black glass, 3.5" x 1.75". $35-45.

Clasps, *Top*: unmarked, c. 1920. Fan of pavé set rhinestones in a brass base with a silver wash, black pressed glass center stone, 2.25 x 2". $15-20. *Bottom*: Unmarked, c. 1910. Ovals of stamped brass, trimmed with rope filigree and bezel set black glass stones centered in the ovals, and bezel set stones joining the clasp, 5.5" x 1.5". $40-50.

Clasp, marked on paper sticker, "Made in Czecho Slovkia," c. 1910. Rectangles of pressed black slag with brass mounts, 1.25" x 1". $20-25.

Clasp, marked "Made in Czecho Slovakia," c. 1910. Rectangles of pressed black glass, with centers of silver trimmed imitation cut steels, with brass mounts, 2.5" x 1". $30-40.

Buckle, marked "Made in Czechoslov," c. 1910. Pressed black glass on opposite corners, prong set rhinestones on opposing corners set in a brass base, 2.25" x 1.5". $25-30.

Clasp, marked "Czechoslovakia," c. 1900. Six sided convexed geometric design of pressed black glass, 3.5" x 1.75". $35-45.

Clasp, marked "Made in Czechoslo-vakia," c. 1910. Circles of pressed black glass trimmed in silver with geometric design and brass mounts, 2" x 1". $25-30.

Buckle, unmarked, c. 1945. Black marbled pressed glass triangles separated by brass beads, divided by white glass beads and a metal bar, 2" x 1.5". $15-20.

Buckle, unmarked, c. 1900. Rectangle of pressed black glass beads mounted on brass plate, 3.75" x 1". $15-20.

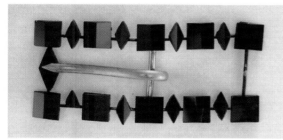

Buckle, unmarked, c. 1880. Geometric designs of pressed black glass mounted on a rectangle wire back, with brass prong, 2.75" x 1.25". $25-30.

Clasp, marked "Czechoslovakia," c. 1910, Rectangles of pressed black glass with gold trim, imitation cut steels and centered geometric glass stones and brass mounts, 3" x .75". $30-35.

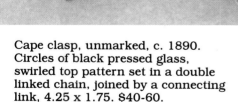

Cape clasp, unmarked, c. 1890. Circles of black pressed glass, swirled top pattern set in a double linked chain, joined by a connecting link, 4.25 x 1.75. $40-60.

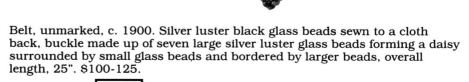

Belt, unmarked, c. 1900. Silver luster black glass beads sewn to a cloth back, buckle made up of seven large silver luster glass beads forming a daisy surrounded by small glass beads and bordered by larger beads, overall length, 25". $100-125.

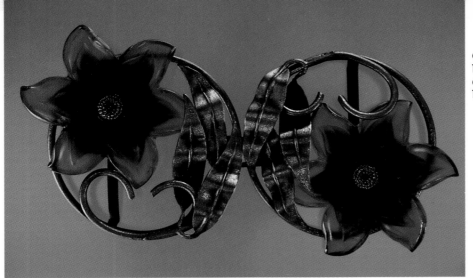

Clasp, unmarked, c. 1950. Transparent brown pressed glass flowers on a brass disc, mounted in a brass ring with long brass leaves, 5.25" x 2.75". $35-50.

Clasp, marked "Made in Cecho.Slov GES.GES," c. 1890. Oblong shaped, green pattern foil under glass set in a brass base, 2.5" x 1.25". $70-90.

Clasp, unmarked, c. 1920. Petal shaped, prong set red glass stones set in a cast base decorated with gold washed stemmed flowers, 4" x 1.75". $30-40. *Connie Fitzner collection.*

Clasps, unmarked, c. 1920. Diamond shaped, bezel set stones set in a brass riveted base, colors shown are cobalt blue, red, amber, and emerald green, 3" x 1.75". $30-40 ea..

Clasp, unmarked, c. 1890. Front and back. Circles of lampwork beads sewed to a brass base, 3.75" x 2". $40-50.

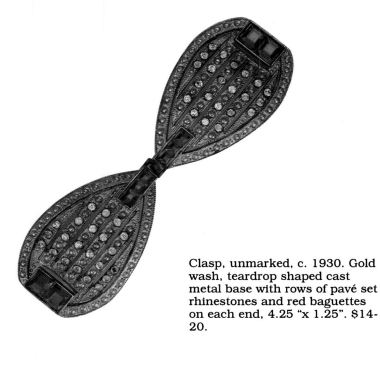

Clasp, unmarked, c. 1910. Square shaped stamped brass filigree base, with prong set picture under glass of Dutch dancing girls, 2.75" x 1.75". $40-50.

Clasp, unmarked, c. 1930. Gold wash, teardrop shaped cast metal base with rows of pavé set rhinestones and red baguettes on each end, 4.25 "x 1.25". $14-20.

Clasp, unmarked, c. 1930. Round shaped, double circles of pavé set rhinestones with violet cabochons between the rows of rhinestones, with large violet slag glass stones in the middle suspended by a single screw mount, 3.25" x 1.75". $30-50.

Clasp, marked "Made in Czechoslovakia," c. 1935. Oval shaped stamped brass base with large blue pressed glass center stones, 3.5" x 1.25". $25-35.

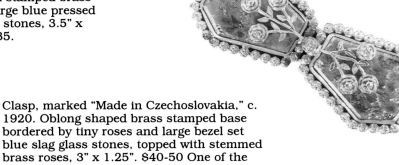

Clasp, marked "Made in Czechoslovakia," c. 1920. Oblong shaped brass stamped base bordered by tiny roses and large bezel set blue slag glass stones, topped with stemmed brass roses, 3" x 1.25". $40-50 One of the authors favorites.

Buckle, slide, unmarked, c. 1925. Oblong shaped, stamped brass base, of classic design, with large rosé colored pressed glass stone, 2.75" x 1.5". $15-20.

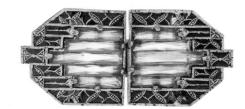

Clasp, unmarked, c. 1920. Rectangular shaped brass filigree base with prong set amber colored pressed glass stones, , 2.5" x 1.25". $25-30.

Clasp, unmarked, c. 1920. Square shaped silver washed brass base with prong set, blue pressed glass center stones, 2.25" x 1". $15-20.

Clasp, marked "Czechoslovakia," c. 1915. Crown shaped brass rope base with prong set rhinestones and large transparent blue cabochons, centered, 2.5" x 1.25". $20-25.

Clasp, unmarked, c. 1920. Classic design, silver washed brass base with pressed transparent blue glass prong set stones, 2" x 1". $25-30.

Buckle, slide, unmarked, c. 1915. Square brass base with filigree trim and prong set rhinestones with amber stones in each corner, 1.25" sq. $20-25.

Clasps, marked "Made in Czechoslovakia," c. 1920. Round brass base with filigree trim, foil under glass. *Left:* amber, *Right:* green, 2.5" x 1.5". $ 30-40.

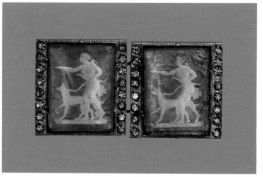

Clasp, unmarked, c. 1900. Square shaped cast base with pavé set rhinestones on the sides, centers of foil under glass, hunter with bow and arrows and dog on leash, white figures with pink background, 2.25" x 1.25". $40-50.

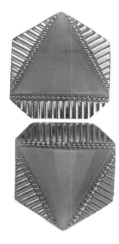

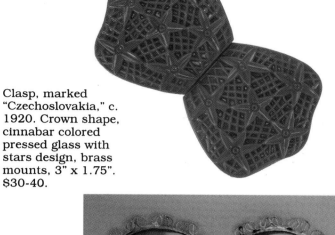

Clasp, marked "Czechoslovakia," c. 1920. Crown shape, cinnabar colored pressed glass with stars design, brass mounts, 3" x 1.75". $30-40.

Clasps, left marked "Czecho Slovakia," right, unmarked, both c. 1910. *Left*: Rectangle shape, pressed transparent glass with gold trim and scroll design, 2.25" x 1.25". $20-25. *Right*: Seven sided, tan, pressed glass with gold trim, 2.75" x 1.25". $20-25.

Clasp, marked "Made in Czechoslovakia," c. 1915. Oval shaped brass base with filigree trim, pressed green slag glass, bezel set, 2.75" x 1.25". $25-30.

Buckle, unmarked, c. 1915. Oblong shape brass rope base with half circles of prong set rhinestones, four larger rhinestones in brass flower petals, 3" x 2". $25-30.

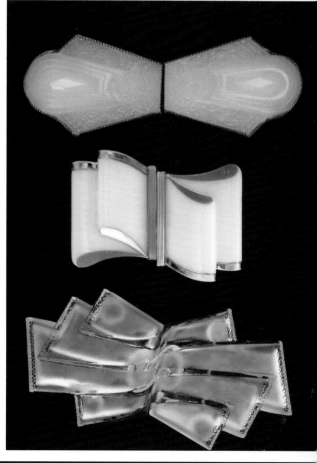

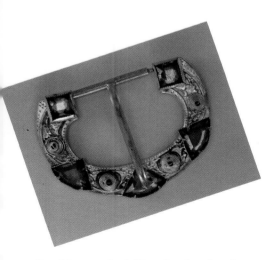

Buckle, marked "Czechoslovakia," c. 1915. Half circle shaped brass filigree base with spirals of rope filigree separating bezel set emerald green rhinestones, 2.5" x 1.5". $25-30.

Clasps, c. 1910. *Top*: Unmarked, oblong shaped pressed milk colored glass with scrolled design, prong set in a metal base with brass mounts, 3.25" x 1.25". $25-30. *Middle*: Unmarked, ribbon shaped white pressed glass with silver trim and brass mounts, 2" x 1.25". $25-30. *Bottom*: Marked "Czechslov," transparent, pressed glass with frosted top ribbon bow design with brass mounts, 3" x 1.75". $30-35.

Buckle, unmarked, c. 1930. Oval shaped cast base with amethyst colored stones, prong set in a leaf arrangement, wire mesh with attachment loop, 5" x 2". $30-50.

Clasp, marked "Czechoslovakia," c. 1910. Circle of prong set rhinestones set in a brass rope base with two blue slag stones, bezel set, 2.25" x 1.75". $75-100.

Clasp, unmarked, c. 1920. Rectangles of transparent blue glass, joined by two large prong set rhinestones in a nickel coated brass base, 3" x 1". $25-35.

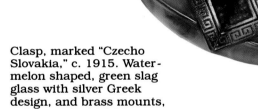

Clasp, unmarked, c. 1920. Red pressed glass geometric design, with gold and silver trim, and brass mount, 2.25" x 1". $25-30.

Clasp, marked "Czecho Slovakia," c. 1915. Water-melon shaped, green slag glass with silver Greek design, and brass mounts, 2.5" x 1.25". $25-30.

Clasp, unmarked, c. 1920. Six sided, concave, pressed red glass, beaded design with brass mount, 2" x 1". $15-20.

Clasp, marked "Czecho Slovkia," c. 1915. Pressed red glasswith angles trimmed in gold and silver with brass mounts, 2.25" x 1". $30-40.

Clasp, marked "Czecho Slovkia," c. 1920. Bow shaped with gold flame design, blue pressed glass with brass mounts, 2.25" x 1". 30-40.

Clasp, marked "Czecho Slovakia,"c. 1910. Six sided, foil under amber glass in a brass base, 2" x 1". $30-40.

Clasp, unmarked, c. 1915. Squares of green pressed glass with Greek design and gold trim with brass mounts, 2.25" x 1.25". $20-25.

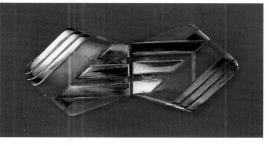

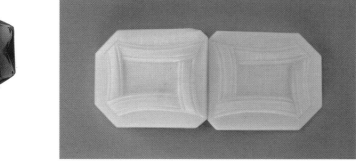

Clasp, marked "Czechoslovakia," c. 1930. Simple design of clear pressed glass with silver trim and brass mounts, 2.5" x 1". $25-30.

Clasp, marked "Czecho Slov," c. 1920. Oblong shaped with marbled green end stones, prong set, with three middle cabochons seperated by two rows of pavé set rhinestones, 2.5" x 1.25". $40-50.

Clasp, marked "Czechoslovakia," c. 1920. Six sided, transparent blue glass stones prong set in a brass base, 2" x 1.25". $20-25.

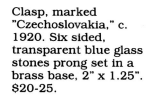

Clasp, marked "Czechoslovakia," c. 1920. Squares of white pressed glass with ribbon design on top and brass mounts, 2.75" x 1.25". $25-30.

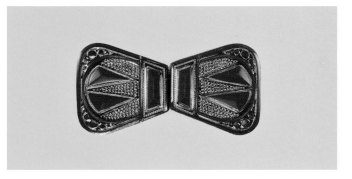

Clasp, front and back, marked with sticker, "Made in Czecho Slovakia," c. 1920. Circles of green pressed glass with raised diamond design on top and brass mounts, 2.25" x 1". $20-30.

Clasp, marked "Czechoslovakia." c. 1920. Bow shaped, blue pressed glass with silver and gold trim on geometric designs with brass mounts, 2" x 1". $25-35.

Clasp, marked "Made in CzechoSlovakia," c. 1920. Bow shaped, pink ribbon glass set in a plated brass base, 2.5" x 1". $30-35.

Clasp, unmarked, c. 1920. Oval base of white pot metal with rows of red and green pavé set rhinestones, large red glass cabochons, fastened with centered cut steels, 4.25" x 1.5". $30-40.

Clasp, marked "Made in Czecho Slovakia," c. 1920. Octagonal shaped, blue pressed glass with ribbon design trimmed in gold with brass mounts, 2.5" x 1.25". $30-40.

Buckle, unmarked, c. 1910. Rectangle, brass base with prong set amethyst colored stones, 1.75" x 1". $15-20.

Clasp, unmarked, c. 1920. Shell shaped, red glass stones set in plated cast base of pavé set rhinestones, 1.5" x 1". $10-15.

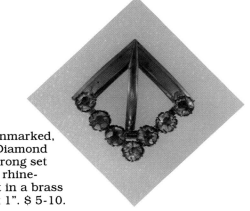

Buckle, unmarked, c. 1930. Diamond shaped, prong set turquoise rhinestones set in a brass base, 1" x 1". $ 5-10.

Buckle, unmarked, c. 1920. Rectangle shaped nickel plated brass base with bezel set rhinestones separating prong set cobalt blue baguettes. Note broken hook., 2.5" x 1.5". $15-20.

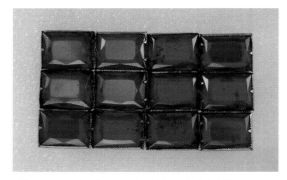

Clasp, marked "Czecho Slovak 31," Rectangles of transparent red glass stones, prong and bezel set in a plated brass base, 2.5" x 1.5". $20-30.

Clasp, unmarked, c. 1915. Oblong shaped rope filigree base, ringed with prong set rhinestones and two large emerald colored stones, bezel set, 2.5" x 1". $40-50.

Clasp, marked "Czechoslovakia," c. 1915. Oblong shaped, emerald and clear rhinestones bezel set in plated brass base, 2.25" x 1.25". $40-50.

Buckle, unmarked, c. 1920. Square brass base with sides of square bezel set amber colored stones, 1.5" x 1.5". $15-25.

Buckle, unmarked, c. 1930. Oval shaped slide, multicolored prong set stones in a plated brass base, 2.75" x 1.75". $10-20.

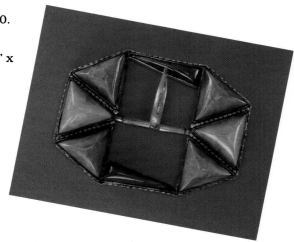

Buckle, unmarked, c. 1920. Eight sided, with pink, blue, and green diamond shaped slag stones bezel set in a brass base, 2.5" x 1.75". $20-30.

Buckle, marked "Czechoslovakia," c. 1910. Oblong shaped with crescents on each end topped with small flowers and bezel set green cabochons, opposite sides are filled with an emerald colored slag glass bezel set in brass base, 2.5"x 2". $30-40.

Buckle, marked "Czechoslovakia," c. 1915. Classic design filigree brass base with prong set red, green, amber, and blue glass, 2.75" x 1.75". $15-25.

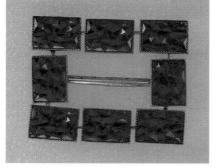

Buckle, marked "Czechoslova-kia," c. 1925. Square shaped brass base with faceted transparent red glass stones, bezel set, 2"x 1.75". $15-20.

Buckle, slide, marked "Made in Czecho-slovakia," c. 1910. Rectangle shaped, bordered with prong set rhinestones with blue slag glass, prong set at each corner, 2" x 1.5". $20-25.

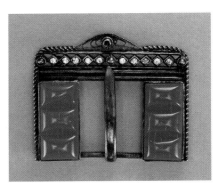

Buckle, marked "Cechoslov." c. 1920. Square shaped silver plated metal base with pavé set rhinestones across the front and pressed red glass along each side, 2" x 1.75". $20-25.

Clasp, unmarked, c. 1920. Leaf shaped gold wash cast base, with brass filigree leaves and multi colored prong set stones, 3.75" x 1.25". $75-100.

Clasp, unmarked, c. 1915. Stamped brass base, bouquet of flowers with multi-colored pressed glass stones bezel set, and centered in each flower, 3" x 2". $70-90.

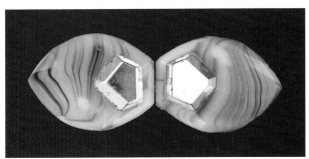

Clasp, unmarked, c. 1910. Teardrop shapes of violet slag glass with five sided mirrors mounted to the center edge, 3" x 1.25". $20-30.

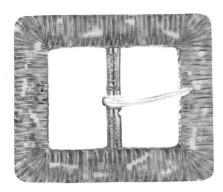

Buckle, marked "Czecho Slovakia," c. 1930. Square shape, patterned clear glass with colors etched in the bottom, single prong closure, 2.25" x 2". $10-15.

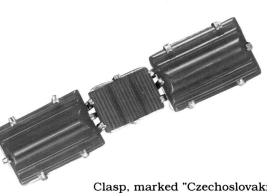

Clasp, marked "Czechoslovakia," c. 1930. Three piece, translucent red pressed glass prong set, rolled pattern, 3.25" x 1". $35-40.

Clasp, unmarked, c. 1900.
Round, white patterned
pressed glass, enameled
outline in a brass filigree base,
3.75" x 1.75". $35-45.

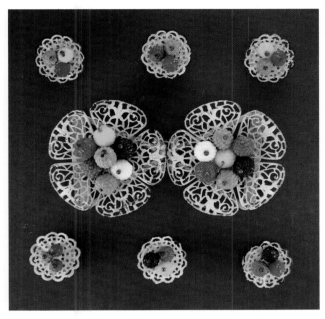

Buckle, unmarked, c. 1930. Three glass oriental figures,
blue and red, in a cast brass base, 3.5" x 1.5". $35-50.
Evelyn Gibbons collection.

Clasp/Buttons set, unmarked, c. 1910. White
enamel on stamped brass filigree, multi-colored
pressed glass beads wired to the base, clasp is 3.5" x
1.75", buttons, .75" dia.. $50-75.

Clasp, marked "Made in Czechoslovakia,"
c. 1925. Greek figures, foil under glass in
a silver on brass base, 2.25" x 1" x .75".
$35-50. *Mrs. W.C. Hewitt collection.*

Clasp and dress clip
set, unmarked, c.
1920. Oxidized,
stamped brass flower
pattern with bezel
set, large red faceted
glass, clasp, 2.5" x
2", clip, 1.25" x
1.75". $50-75.

Clasp/Chain button set, unmarked, c. 1900. Circles of oblong and round multi-colored glass beads wired and sewn to a perforated brass disc, with a metal button at center. 3.5" x 1.75". Buttons are oblong multi-colored glass separated by metal plates, wired together and joined by a chain, .75" x 1". $50-75.

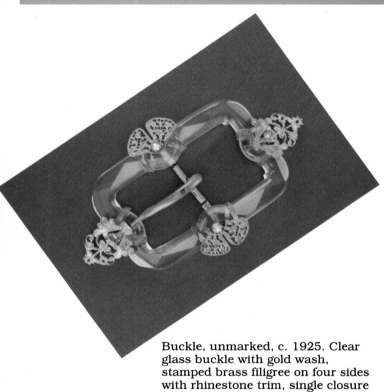

Buckle, unmarked, c. 1925. Clear glass buckle with gold wash, stamped brass filigree on four sides with rhinestone trim, single closure prong, 3.25" x 2". $35-50.

Clasp, buckles and buttons, card is marked "Nouveauté", c. 1930. Salesman's sample card, pieces are marked, "Czecho Slovakia." Caramel colored glass buckle with rhinestones on each corner with silver trim. Black glass buttons with silver trim and a single rhinestone. Clear glass buckle, round shape. Red, green, brown, and black clasps, matching buttons. $75-100.

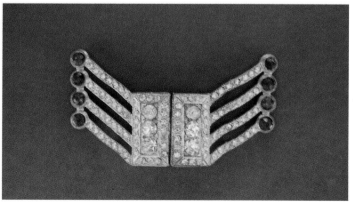

Clasp, marked, c. 1935. Cast base metal, wings of pavé set rhinestones tipped in blue paste, 2.5" x 1.5". $20-25.

Chapter Two
Buckles Made From Metal

Metal buckles is the largest chapter in this book. You'll actually find a bit of all the materials in this chapter, but if the primary material of a piece is metal, it will be found here. We have included enamel buckles in this chapter for that very reason.

Metal buckles come in a vast array of metals and combinations of materials. They can be found made out of aluminum, silver, pewter, copper, brass, steel and tin.

Steel

Steel is a hard metal composed of iron alloyed with carbon and sometimes with other metals. It is often used as a base material, but can also be found as an adornment on other materials. Steel has a tendency to rust and should be handled as little as possible and stored in dry conditions.

The most common use of steel is in cut steels, where individual faceted steel pieces are riveted onto metal backs. Matthew Boulton of Birmingham, England invented the cut-steel process in the middle of the eighteenth century and it became popular in women's fashions in the nineteenth century. A less expensive manufacturing technique of cut-steels involved stamping a sheet of steel to imitate the riveted process. It was invented by M. Trichot in the early part of the nineteenth century. Steel was sometimes tinted with a metal oxide dye to produce a wide range of colors. The dye also helped to prevent rusting.

Brass

Brass is an alloy of copper and zinc which became popular during the eighteenth century for making jewelry and was probably the most frequently used metal in buckle manufacturing. It has been cast, stamped, plated, engraved, oxidized and gilded.

Enamel

Enameling is the process of applying a fine powder or paste of glass to a metal surface, usually in pattern form. After the design is complete, heat is applied to melt the glass and fuse it to the metal base. There are several different enameling techniques, of which, three are shown in this book. The oldest method is cloisonné, where thin wires or bands of metal are used to form a design that is then soldered to the base metal. The spaces or cloisons are then filled with powdered colored enamel. The buckle is then heated in an oven until the powder is reduced to a glass-like substance.

Champlevé is somewhat like cloisonné, but instead of a pattern of fine wire, the design is carved or stamped out of a single piece of metal.

A refined form of champlevé enameling, *basse taille*, was developed in the thirteenth century. Translucent colors were used over a design in low relief in which the base metal pattern could be seen through the enamel coating.

Clasp, tinted steel discs fastened to a metal back plate with a screen mesh center, fastened by small faceted cut steels, 3" x 1.5". $20-30.

Clasp, marked "Brevete S.G.D.G. Déposé," c. 1915. Rectangle shaped, plated metal with rows of faceted cut steels riveted to a plate, and riveted to the back plate, 3.25" x 1.75". $80-90.

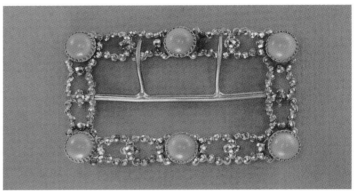

Clasp, faceted cut steels riveted to a gold washed brass base of flower design, 3.5" x 2". $40-50.

Buckle, late Victorian. Rectangle shaped, circles of small faceted steels, six turquoise blue cabochons, bezel set, and riveted to a brass base, plated metal bar with two closure hooks, 2.75" x 1.5". $50-70.

Buckle, c. 1890. Rectangle shaped, gold wash on brass base with faceted steels riveted to two sides, double prong closures, 2" x 1.25". $20-30.

Buckle, c. 1825-1900. Trichot method of stamped facsimile of cut steels, with faceted steels riveted to a brass base with single prong closure, 3.75" x 3". $40-50.

Clasp, c. 1825-1900. Trichot method of stamped pattern facsimile of cut steels with four quarter moon shaped steels riveted to a stamped brass base, 1.5" x 1.25". $20-30.

Clasp, c. 1910. Plated stamped pattern facsimile of cut steels attached to a steel back plate, 5" x 1.75". $20-30.

Clasp, c. 1880-1900. Butterfly pattern, polished cut steels riveted to a brass base, 2.5" x 2.25". $70-90.

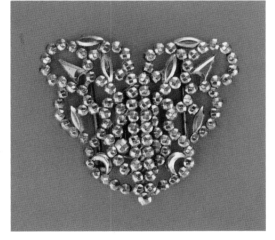

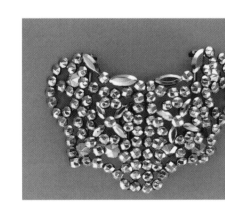

Clasp, c. 1880-1900. Wing pattern, polished cut steels riveted to a brass base, 2.5" x 1.75". $70-90.

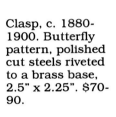
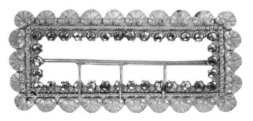

Buckle, c. 1900. Ornate stamped brass base with triple prong closure inside border of small faceted cut steels, 3" x 1.25". $20-30.

Buckle, c. 1880-1900. Square with double prong closure, four rows of faceted steels riveted to a brass base, 3.25" sq. $25-30.

Buckle, c. 1900. Oval shaped, stamped pattern facsimile of cut steel riveted to a gold washed base plate with four faceted cut steels, 3" x 2". $20-25.

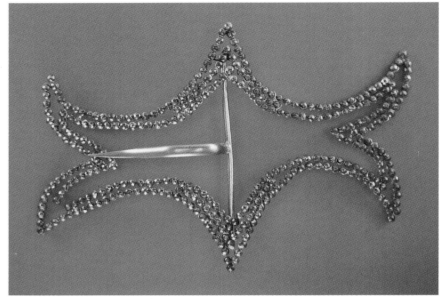

Buckle, sash, c. 1880-1900. Large six pointed, flared with double rows of faceted steels riveted to a plated brass base with a single closure prong, 8.5" x 2.5". $60-80.

Buckle, slide, c. 1900. Rectangle shaped, figure eight of small faceted steels bordered by pyramid shaped steels, riveted to a brass base, single mount bar, 3.25" x 1.25". $25-35.

Buckle, sash, c. 1880-1900. Rectangle shaped, scalloped rows of faceted cut steels tinted by the use of metal oxide dyes in blue, red and gold, riveted to a brass base with a five prong closure, 5.5" x 1.75". $70-90.

Buckle, slide, c. 1900. Rectangle shaped, rows of small coins fastened to brass bars with scallops of small faceted steels riveted to a brass base, 4.5" x 1.25". $30-40.

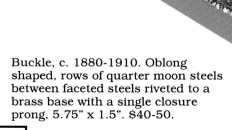

Buckle, c. 1880-1910. Oblong shaped, rows of quarter moon steels between faceted steels riveted to a brass base with a single closure prong, 5.75" x 1.5". $40-50.

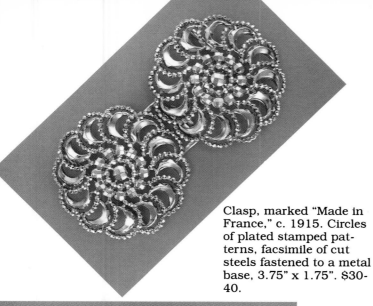

Clasp, marked "Made in France," c. 1915. Circles of plated stamped patterns, facsimile of cut steels fastened to a metal base, 3.75" x 1.75". $30-40.

Clasp, c. 1880-1900. Flower shaped, faceted cut steels riveted to a brass base, 2.75" x 2.25". $70-80.

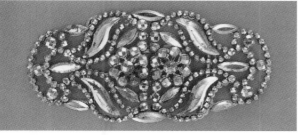

Clasp, c. 1825-1900. Trichot method of stamped facsimile cut steels riveted to a brass base with faceted steels, 3" x 1.5". $40-50.

Clasp, c. 1910. Heart shaped pattern of facsimile cut steels fastened to a stamped brass base, 3" x 2.25". $20-30.

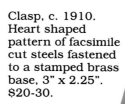

Clasp, c. 1900. Scalloped circles of stamped patterns of facsimile cut steels fastened to a brass base by riveted, faceted, and quarter moon shaped steels, 2.5" x 2". $40-50.

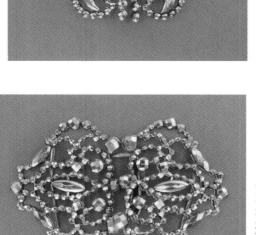

Clasp, c. 1900. Patterned shapes of facsimile cut steels fastened to a brass base by faceted steels, 2.5" x 1.75". $25-30.

Buckle, c. 1890. Circle of paisley shapes highlighted with red and green rhinestones and tiny faceted cut steels, riveted to a metal base, dia.3.5". $55-75.

Buckle, slide, c. 1890. Oblong shape of stamped faceted steels surrounding large steels in a paisley pattern, riveted to a felt covered metal base, 5" x 2.25". $60-70. *Connie Fitzner collection.*

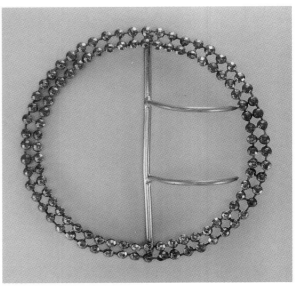

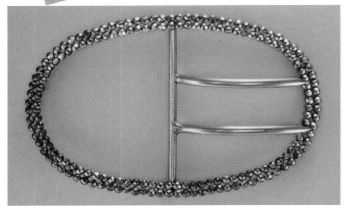

Buckle, c. 1900. Round shaped, stamped pattern of cut steels riveted to a brass base with faceted cut steels, double prong closure, dia. 3". $25-35.

Buckle, c. 1850-1900. Round shaped, double row of faceted cut steels riveted to a brass base with double prong closure, dia.3.5". $20-30.

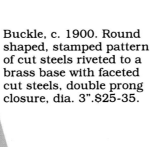

Buckle, c. 1850-1900. Oblong shaped, double row of faceted cut steels riveted to a brass base with a double prong closure, 3.5" x 2.25". $30-35.

Buckle, c. 1850-1900.00 Tapered double circle of faceted cut steels, separated by larger faceted steels riveted to a brass base with a double prong closure, 1.75" x 1.5". $15-25.

Buckle, c. 1850-1900. Trichot method of stamped facsimile of cut steels riveted to a brass base with faceted steels, joined by prong set rhinestones single prong closure, 3.5" x 2.5". $35-45.

Buckle, c. 1850-1900. Oblong shaped, double row of faceted cut steels riveted to a plated brass base with double prong closure, 1.75" x 1.5". $15-25.

Buckle, c. 1850-1900. Square shaped, circles of faceted cut steels, riveted to a brass base with a single prong closure, 2.25" x 2". $25-30.

Buckle, belt and collar, c. 1890-1915. Three round circles of faceted cut steels riveted to a plated metal base, buckle has a facsimile of a closure prong made of steels, rare, dia. 2.25". $45-55.

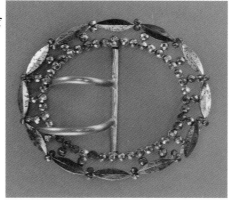

Buckle, c. 1850-1900. Oblong, double circle of faceted cut steels riveted to a plated brass base with a double prong closure, 2.5" x 2.25". $30-40.

Buckle, c. 1880-1900. Clover leave shaped, stamped facsimile of cut steels riveted to a brass base by faceted cut steels, 1.75" x 1.75". $15-25.

Buckle, c. 1880-1900. Oval circles of large and small steels riveted to a brass base with a double prong closure, 2.25" x 1.5". $20-30.

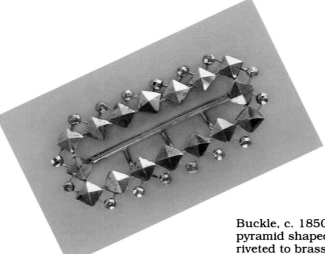

Buckle, c. 1850-1900. Rectangle shaped, rows of larger pyramid shaped steels bordered by faceted cut steels riveted to brass base with three prong closure, 2.75" x 1.25". $25-35.

Buckles, c. 1850-1900. *Top*: Rectangle shaped, larger faceted cut steels separated by doubles of tiny faceted cut steels riveted to a plated brass base with three prong closure, 1.75" x 1". $20-30. *Bottom*: Rectangle shaped, three rows of faceted cut steels riveted to a brass base with three prong closure, 2.5" x 1.25". $20-30.

Buckles, c. 1850-1900. *Left*: Rectangle shaped, double row of faceted cut steels riveted to a brass base with a single closure, 1" x .75". $10-20. *Top*: Oval shaped, double row of gold, red, blue and green faceted cut steels riveted to a brass base with a double closure, 1" x .75". $15-25. *Bottom*: Oval shaped, pyramid shaped steels separated by tiny faceted cut steels riveted to a brass base with a double prong closure, 1.25" x .75". $10-20. *Right*: Rectangle shaped, single row of faceted cut steels riveted to a brass base with double prong closure, 1.25" x .75". $10-20.

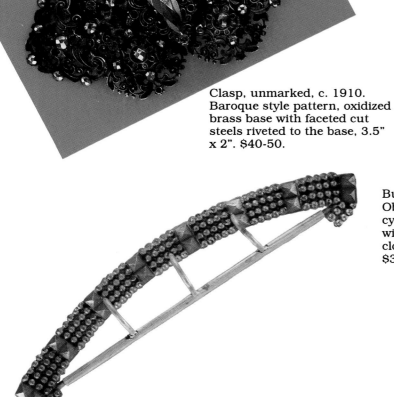

Clasp, unmarked, c. 1910. Baroque style pattern, oxidized brass base with faceted cut steels riveted to the base, 3.5" x 2". $40-50.

Buckle, unmarked, c. 1890. Oblong, pewter wheat with cycles mounted to a brass plate with faceted cut steels, five closure prongs, 5.5" x 1.5". $35-50.

Buckle, unmarked, c. 1910. Imitation cut steels, curved shaped, cast pewter with three prong closure, 5" x 1". $35-40.

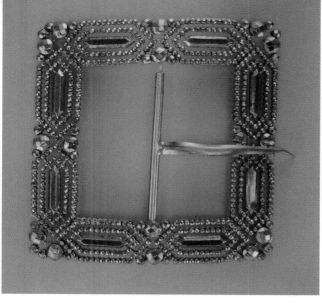

Buckle, c. 1890. Square shaped, small and large faceted steels riveted to a metal base with a single closure hook, 3" x 3". $70-80.

Clasp. Faceted, polished, and gunmetal blue steels riveted to a brass surface, 2.5" x 1.25". $25-35.

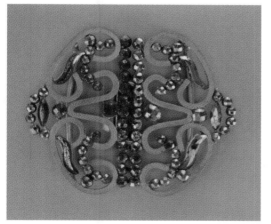

Clasp, c. 1880. Brass rope intertwined around faceted steels, riveted to the brass base, 2.5" x 2". $70-90.

Clasp, late Victorian. Banana shaped brass attached to a brass base, bordered by faceted steels riveted to the base, 2.75" x 2". $80-100.

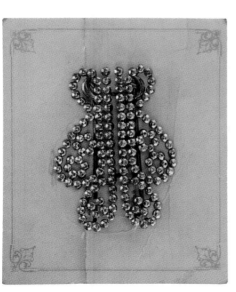

Clasp, unmarked, c. 1900. Faceted, cut steels on a brass base hearts design, on original card, with simple red tracing, clasp, 2" x 2.75". Card is 3.75"x 4.5". $75-100.

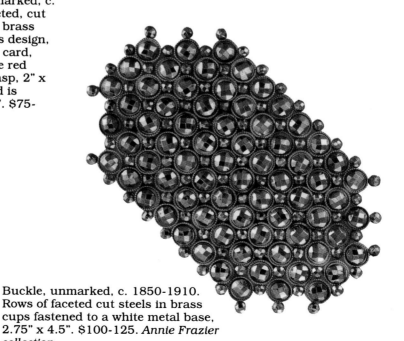

Buckle, unmarked, c. 1850-1910. Rows of faceted cut steels in brass cups fastened to a white metal base, 2.75" x 4.5". $100-125. *Annie Frazier collection.*

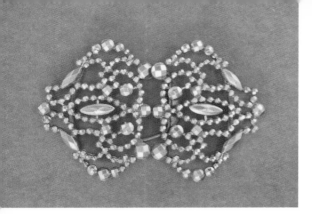

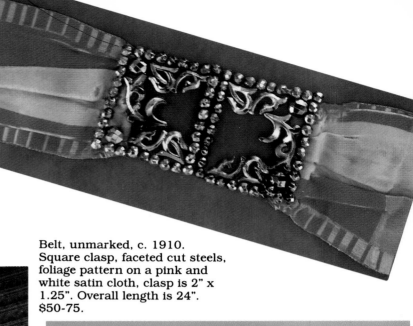

Clasp, unmarked, c. 1850-1910. Imitation cut steels riveted to a brass base with faceted cut steels, 2.75" x 1.75". $35-50. $35-50.

Belt, unmarked, c. 1910. Square clasp, faceted cut steels, foliage pattern on a pink and white satin cloth, clasp is 2" x 1.25". Overall length is 24". $50-75.

Belt, unmarked, c. 1900. Faceted cut steels with a heart pattern fastened to a black elastic cloth, buckle is 4.5" x 2.25". Overall length is 33". $50-75.

Clasp, unmarked, c. 1920. Imitation cut steel, stamped brass pattern fastened to a plated metal back, prong set blue cabochon at center, 4" x 1.75". $25-35.

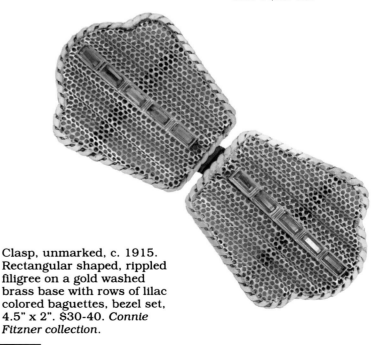

Buckle, unmarked, c. 1850-1910. Rectangular, faceted cut steels riveted to a brass rope design base, four prong closure, 3.5" x 1.5". $50-75.

Clasp, unmarked, c. 1915. Rectangular shaped, rippled filigree on a gold washed brass base with rows of lilac colored baguettes, bezel set, 4.5" x 2". $30-40. *Connie Fitzner collection.*

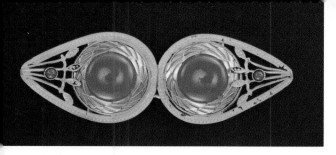

Clasp, marked "Czech.Slovak," c. 1910. Tear drop shaped, brass stemmed flowers with small red cabochons bezel set, large red glass cabochons bezel set, in gold and silver plated leaves in a gold washed brass base, 3.25" x 1.25". $35-45.

Clasp, marked "Hecho en Mexico Btnncourt," c. 1935. Shape of fish with hook in mouth, brass fish with red, green, and black pressed glass cabochons, hook attaches to gill of fish , 7.25" x 2". $50-60.

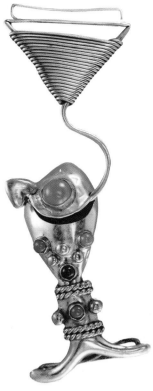

Clasp, unmarked, c. 1910. Baroque style brass stamped pattern, gold washed, goldstone flecked pressed blue glass, bezel set, 2.75" x 2.5". $50-60.

Clasp, unmarked, c. 1900. Circles of scalloped flowers with a large faceted black pressed glass stone, bezel set, in a brass base, 4.55" x 2.25". $40-50.

Clasp, unmarked, c. 1940. Baroque style, stamped brass base with two large and two small imitation turquoise cabochons, bezel set, in circles of imitation beads, 5.25" x 2". $30-40.

Clasp, unmarked, c. 1920. Stamped pattern of stemmed leaves in a silver coated brass base with prong set rhinestones and a center rosette, 5.5" 1.75". $40-50.

Clasp, unmarked, c. 1910. Intricate stamped brass pattern of leaves and flowers, silver coated with four prong set emerald green faceted glass stones, 4.5" x 2". $50-60

Clasp, marked "C & R," c. 1930. Leave shaped, cast oxidized metal, flowers with stems and leaves, imitation amethyst bezel set glass centered, 4" x 1.75". $60-70.

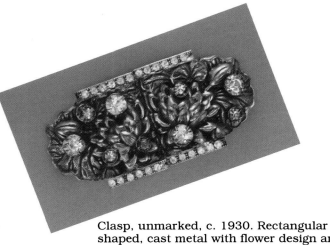

Clasp, unmarked, c. 1930. Rectangular shaped, cast metal with flower design and prong set rhinestones centered on flowers, 2.75" 1.25". $30-35.

Clasp, unmarked, c. 1920. Stamped metal filigree circles of petaled flowers with brilliant blue rhinestones attached to the center of the flowers, 3.25" x 2". $40-50.

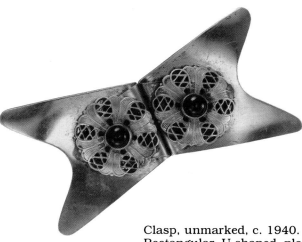

Clasp, unmarked, c. 1940. Rectangular, U shaped, plated metal with a black cabochon bezel set and centered on a filigree rosette, 3.5" x 1.75". $25-30.

Clasp, unmarked, c. 1925. Silver plated shaped leaves with a cluster of seven prong set rhinestones on each leaf, joined by a perforated metal ring, 3.25" x 1.25". $30-35.

Buckle, unmarked, c. 1925. Oval shaped stamped brass base with gold wash, ribbon and flower, with amethyst bezel set paste stones, imitation hasp, 2.25" x 2". $30-35.

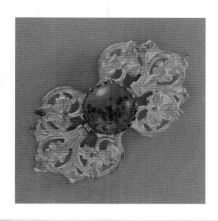

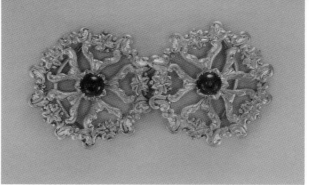

Clasp, unmarked, c. 1920. Stamped brass, flowered pattern with an aquamarine gold flecked cabochon, bezel set, 2.25" x 1.25". $20-25.

Clasp, unmarked, c. 1925. Stamped brass circles of flowers with a prong set blue cabochon, 3" x 1.5". $15-20.

Clasp, marked "Czecho Slovakia," c. 1915. Circles of gold washed stamped brass with three amber colored glass stones, bezel set, 2.5" x 1.25". $30-40.

Clasp, marked "Czechslov," c. 1900. Gold washed brass filigree with three green cabochons, 2.75" x 1.25". $30-40.

Clasp, unmarked, c. 1910. Stamped brass shield with flower pattern and a single prong set imitation amethyst stone, centered, 2.5" x 2.25". $35-40.

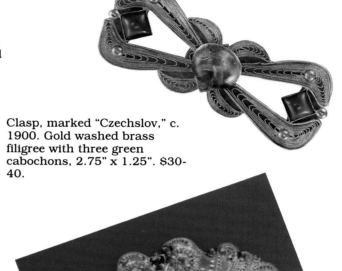

Clasp, unmarked, c. 1925. Stamped brass pattern of feathers and flowers with a bezel set red pressed glass stone, 3" x 1.5". $30-40.

Clasp, unmarked, c. 1920. Triangle shape stamped pattern with bezel set amber colored cabochons, 2.5" x 1". $25-30.

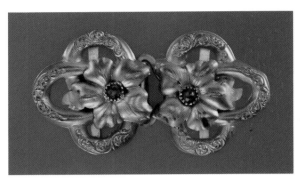

Clasp, unmarked, c. 1929. Stamped brass gold washed flowers surrounded by vines with red paste stones, bezel set, in flower centers, 2.75" x 1.5". $20-25.

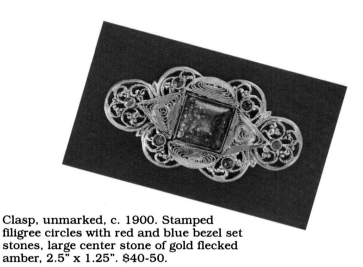

Clasp, unmarked, c. 1900. Stamped filigree circles with red and blue bezel set stones, large center stone of gold flecked amber, 2.5" x 1.25". $40-50.

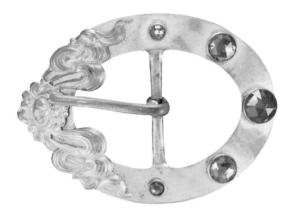

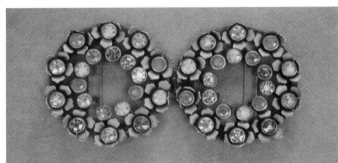

Clasp, unmarked, c. 1915. Circles of flowers with centers of multi-colored bezel set stones riveted to a brass base, 3" x 1.5". $60-70.

Buckle, unmarked, c. 1900. Oval shaped with single closure prong, gold washed Art Nouveau with bezel set rose colored paste stones, 3.25" x 2.5". $50-60

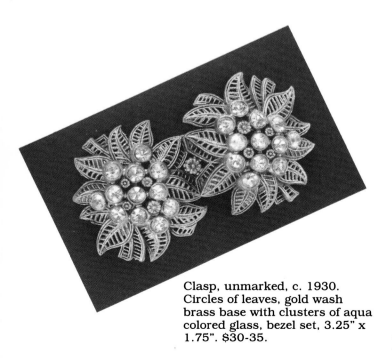

Clasp, unmarked, c. 1930. Circles of leaves, gold wash brass base with clusters of aqua colored glass, bezel set, 3.25" x 1.75". $30-35.

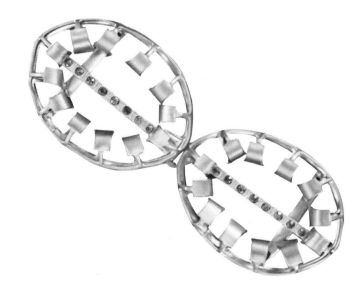

Clasp, unmarked, c. 1935. Oval shaped plated brass base with pavé set aqua colored glass in center cross bar, 4.5" x 1.75". $20-25.

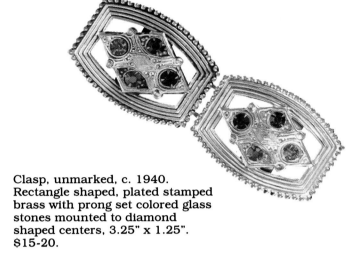

Clasp, unmarked, c. 1900. Stamped plated brass baroque style with a blue prong set cabochon, centered, 3.25" x 1.75. $30-40.

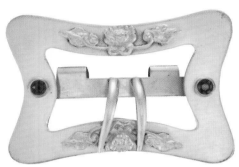

Buckle, unmarked, c. 1910. Rectangle shaped with imitation hasp, gold wash Art Nouveau style with bezel set ruby red glass on each side, 2.75" x 1.75". $40-50.

Clasp, unmarked, c. 1940. Rectangle shaped, plated stamped brass with prong set colored glass stones mounted to diamond shaped centers, 3.25" x 1.25". $15-20.

Buckle, unmarked, 1900. Oval shaped with imitation hasp, cast brass base with vines and leaves and a bezel set, green and white stone, 3" x 2.25". $60-70.

Clasp, unmarked, c. 1910. Gold washed stamped brass triangles of flowers with multi-colored bezel set cabochons, in the flower centers, 3.5" x 2.5". $40-60.

Buckle, unmarked, c. 1900. Rectangle shaped gold washed, stamped brass, single prong closure, fancy feather design with Roman coins top and bottom centered, three prong set rhinestones on each end, 3" x 2". $55-65.

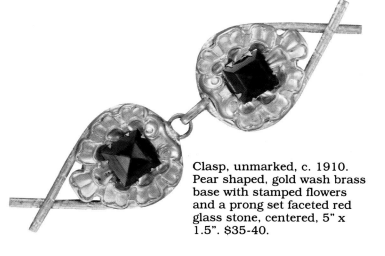

Clasp, unmarked, c. 1910. Pear shaped, gold wash brass base with stamped flowers and a prong set faceted red glass stone, centered, 5" x 1.5". $35-40.

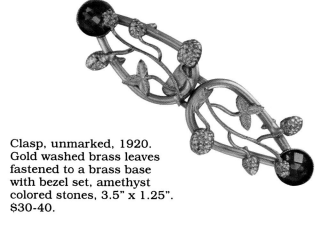

Clasp, unmarked, 1920. Gold washed brass leaves fastened to a brass base with bezel set, amethyst colored stones, 3.5" x 1.25". $30-40.

Clasp, unmarked, c. 1915. Gold washed stamped brass pattern with a single prong set, pink stone, 2.75"x 1.75". $30-40.

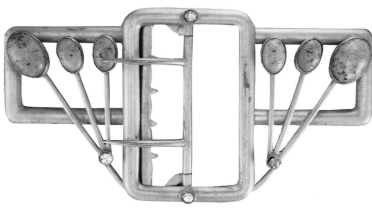

Buckle, marked "7757," c. 1900. Rectangle shaped with double prong closure, gold wash brass with imitation turquoise stones bezel set, on brass stems, and prong set rhinestones, 4.5" x 2.5". $50-55.

Clasp, unmarked, c. 1910. Stamped brass pattern with bezel set, imitation Jade, 3.5" x 2.25". $30-40.

Clasp, unmarked, c. 1915. Stamped brass ribbons of flowers with an imitation bezel set stone, centered on clasp, 4" x 2.5". $35-40.

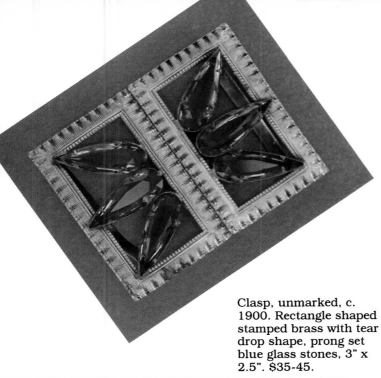

Clasp, unmarked, c. 1925. Metal circles with bezel set pressed glass on top and bottom edge and bezel set black glass in a diamond design, centered on clasp, 3.5" x 2.5". $30-50.

Clasp, unmarked, c. 1900. Rectangle shaped stamped brass with tear drop shape, prong set blue glass stones, 3" x 2.5". $35-45.

Clasp, unmarked, c. 1910. Oblong shaped cast base, flower design with multi-colored paste, bezel set, 3.5" x 1.75". $35-45.

Clasp, unmarked, c. 1910. Oval shaped cast bronze oxide base, bouquets of flowers with multi-colored stones for flower centers, 3.5" x 2". $30-40.

Clasp, unmarked, c. 1900. Oval shaped large red faceted glass bezel set, with prong set amber and green stones in the corners, 3.25" x 1.25". $30-35.

Clasp, marked "WMC 8," c. 1930. Shell shaped cast base metal, with pavé set blue, green, red , and pink glass, 2.25" x 1.25". $30-35.

Clasp, marked "Pat apld for, g," c. 1915. Ribbon shape shield with entwining serpent, Art Nouveau, brass base, 3.25" x 2.25". $50-65.

Buckle, unmarked, c. 1900. Art Nouveau style silver on base metal, head with flowing hair and hand holding flower, 4" x 2". $90-110.

Buckle, unmarked, 1890. Triangle shaped gold washed brass base with filigree trim, double prong closure, 4" x 4" x 3.75". $75-80.

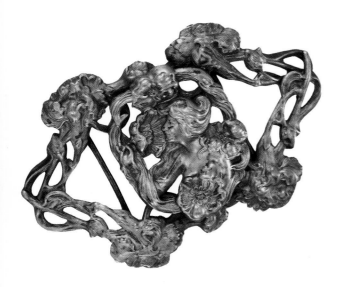

Buckle, slide, unmarked, c. 1900. Art Nouveau style base metal, bust of woman with flowing hair surrounded by flowers, 4" x 2.75". $75-100.

Buckle, slide, unmarked, c. 1900. Art Nouveau style base metal, head of woman between wings over flowers, 4.75" x 2". $75-100.

Buckle, slide, unmarked, c. 1900. Art Nouveau style base metal, head of woman mounted on bamboo style frame, 5" x 2". $75-100.

Clasp, unmarked, c. 1910. Rectangle shaped silver filigree with imitation metal seed pearls, 3.25" x 1". $35-40.

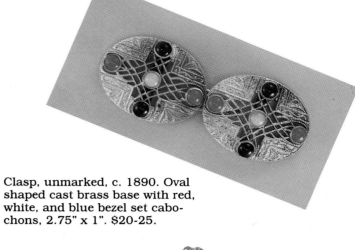

Clasp, unmarked, c. 1890. Oval shaped cast brass base with red, white, and blue bezel set cabochons, 2.75" x 1". $20-25.

Clasp, marked "81 Czecho Slovakia," c. 1890. Triangle shaped brass filigree base with an emerald green paste stone between two bezel set marcasites, joined by a bezel set blue slag cabochon, 2.5" x 1.5". $50-60.

Clasp, unmarked, c. 1910. Square shaped stamped brass base, flowers at corners, center is amber foil under glass, 2.75" x 1.25". $20-30.

Clasp, unmarked, c. 1920. Circles linked together, cast base with multi-colored stones, pavé set, 3" x 1.5". $25-30.

Clasp, unmarked, c. 1920. Triangle shaped, cast base metal gold washed, with multi-colored pavé set stones, with four colored baguettes at each end, 3.25" x 1.5". $20-30.

Clasp, unmarked, c. 1900. Round shaped cast brass base with red and white bezel set, slag stones, 2.5" x 1.25". $15-25.

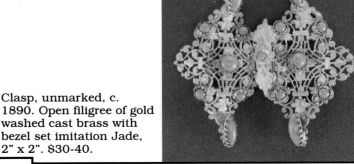

Clasp, unmarked, c. 1890. Open filigree of gold washed cast brass with bezel set imitation Jade, 2" x 2". $30-40.

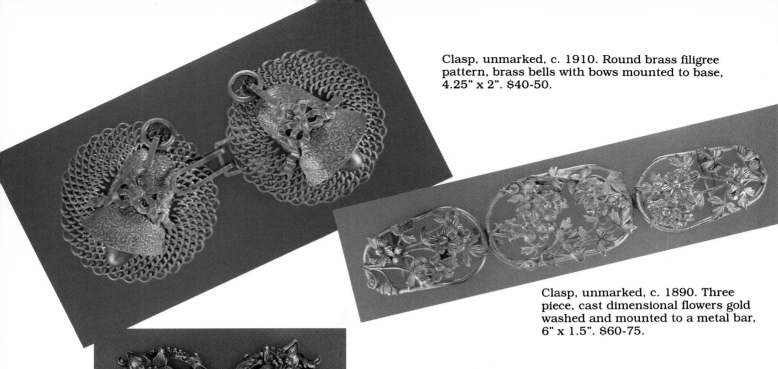

Clasp, unmarked, c. 1910. Round brass filigree pattern, brass bells with bows mounted to base, 4.25" x 2". $40-50.

Clasp, unmarked, c. 1890. Three piece, cast dimensional flowers gold washed and mounted to a metal bar, 6" x 1.5". $60-75.

Clasp, unmarked, c. 1900. Brass base, gold wash with raised stemmed flowers with leaves, 2.75" x 2.75". $50-75.

Clasp, unmarked, c. 1900. Art Nouveau style flowers, stamped white base metal with a bezel set, mother of pearl button, 3" x 2". $50-75.

Clasp, unmarked, c. 1900. Stemmed roses in a stamped brass base with a vase center piece, 2.75" x 2". $40-50.

Clasp, unmarked, c. 1885. Edwardian style brass stamped pattern, 3.5" x 2.75". $50-75.

Clasp, unmarked, c. 1900. Gold wash brass base with large pansy at center, 3" x 2". $30-35.

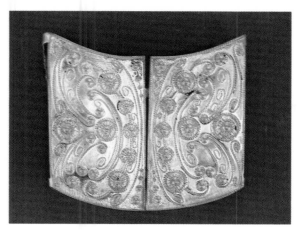

Clasp, unmarked, c. 1880. Gold washed stamped pattern, brass shields, 2.5" x 2". $30-40

Clasp, unmarked, c. 1920. Art Nouveau, die cut flower pattern, 3.25" x 2.25". $30-40.

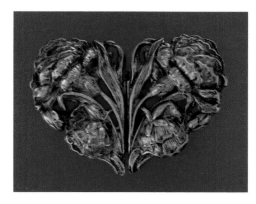

Clasp, unmarked, c. 1910. Flowers with stems, stamped brass, 2.5" x 1.75". $30-40.

Clasp, unmarked, c. 1915. Gold washed stamped brass with paisley design, 3.5" x 2". $30-40.

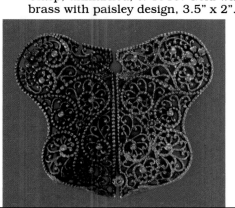

Clasp, unmarked, c. 1890. Stamped flower design, oxidized base metal, 3.75" x 2". $30-40.

Clasp, unmarked, c. 1915. Cast base metal, pierced pattern with flowers, 2.5"x 2.25". $25-35.

Clasp, unmarked, c. 1910. Stamped pattern of roses, oxidized brass metal, large faceted amethyst stone bezel set and centered on oval plate, 3" x 2.25". $50-60.

Clasp, unmarked, c. 1900. Silver on brass stamped roses with leaves, fastened to ovals and joined at the middle, 3" x 1.75". $75-100.

Clasp, unmarked, c. 1900. Baroque style silver on brass, stamped base, 2.5" x 1.25". $25-35.

Clasp, unmarked, c. 1920. Flowers on leaves with vine, gold washed brass base, 4" x 2". $30-40.

Clasp, unmarked, c. 1920. Pansies set in a circle of stems and leaves, gold washed stamped brass base, 3.75" x 2.25". $30-40.

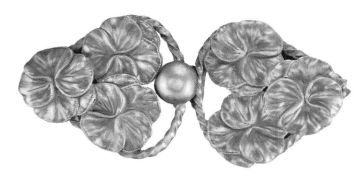

Clasp, unmarked, c. 1915. Overlapping flowers on a rope base, oxidized stamped brass base, 4.25" x 1.75". $30-40

Clasp, unmarked, c. 1920. Water lilies with leaves in circle of vines, gold wash brass base, 3" x 2". $35-45.

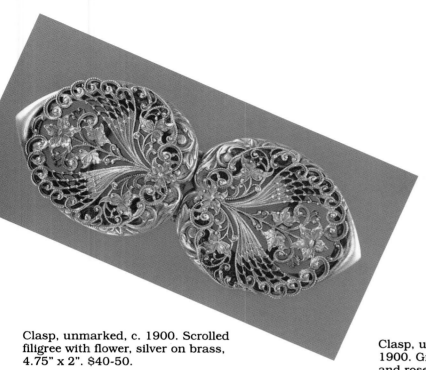

Clasp, unmarked, c. 1920. Large pansy on a gold washed stamped brass base, 3.75" x 1.75". $30-40.

Clasp, unmarked, c. 1900. Scrolled filigree with flower, silver on brass, 4.75" x 2". $40-50.

Clasp, unmarked, c. 1900. Greek figures and roses, silver on brass, 2.5" x 2". $50-75.

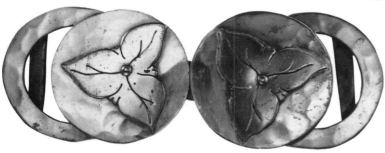

Clasp, unmarked, c. 1950. Circles of copper with brass leaves, 5.25" x 2". $30-40.

Clasp, unmarked, c. 1925. Gold washed filigree, imitation pearls on flower centers, 3" x 2". $30-40.

Clasp, marked "312," c. 1920. Scalloped ovals of gold washed filigree with flower pattern, 4" x 2.25". $40-50.

Clasp, unmarked, c. 1930. Art Deco, oxidized brass stamped leaves with pavé set rhinestones across the center, 5" x 2.25". $25-30.

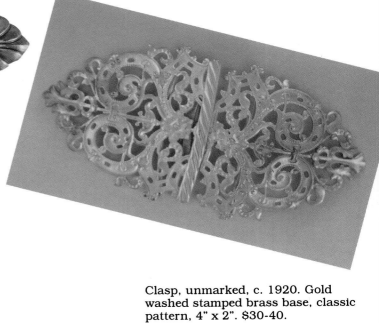

Clasp, unmarked, c. 1920. Gold washed stamped brass base, classic pattern, 4" x 2". $30-40.

Clasp, unmarked, c. 1890. Ovals of brass roping, stamped brass coils across ovals, 5.5" x 1.5". $40-50.

Clasp, unmarked, c. 1940. Art Deco, silver on brass with black trim, circled ropes with wings, 5" 1.75".$20-30.

Buckle, unmarked, c. 1880. Rectangle, silver on brass with flower head by a scalloped stamped pattern, double prong closure, 5" x 1.5". $75-100.

Clasp, unmarked, c. 1900. Stamped rose pattern, oxidized brass base, 4.25" x 2.25". $35-40.

Clasp, hallmark "E & Co.," c. 1905. Cast silver medallion of Sara Bernhardt as L'Aiglon, (Little Eaglet), 2.75" x 1.5". $100-125.

Clasp, unmarked, c. 1890. Woman with lyre, silver on brass, 4" x 1.75". $35-50.

Clasp, unmarked, c. 1900. Hammered brass discs with cast stag head, chain with metal ball trim, 2.5" x 1.25". $30-35.

Clasp, marked "C&R," c. 1910. Oval shaped, cast silver on brass with bezel set, imitation amethyst on each half with flower, 2" x 1.75". $75-100.

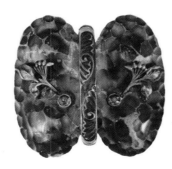

Buckle, marked"C&R," c. 1910. Rectangle, stamped silver on brass oval pattern of flowers, open center, 3.25" x 2". $75-100.

Buckle, marked "35," c. 1910. German, round stamped metal, German nickel, scroll pattern on each side, 3" dia.. $30-35.

Buckle, unmarked, c. 1915. German, oxidized stamped metal pattern, 2.5" x 2". $30-35.

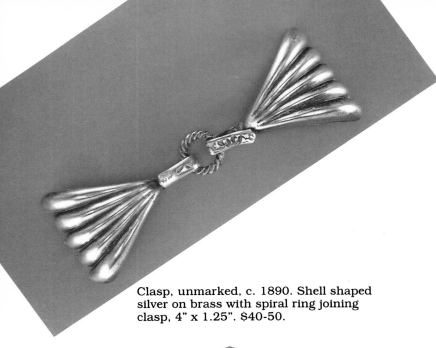

Clasp, unmarked, c. 1890. Shell shaped silver on brass with spiral ring joining clasp, 4" x 1.25". $40-50.

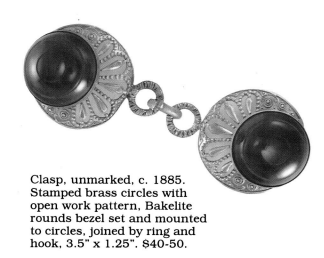

Clasp, unmarked, c. 1885. Stamped brass circles with open work pattern, Bakelite rounds bezel set and mounted to circles, joined by ring and hook, 3.5" x 1.25". $40-50.

Clasp, unmarked, c. 1930. Triangle shaped silver on metal, torch mounted to each half with metal ball at tip, 4.5" x 1.5". $15-25.

Clasp, unmarked, c. 1900. Queen Liliuokaliai, cast base metal figure on brass mounted to plated metal base with flower trim, 3.75" x 1.75". $50-75.

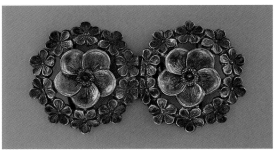

Clasp, unmarked, 1910. Large posy surrounded by smaller posies, oxidized stamped brass, 2.5" x 1.25". $20-30.

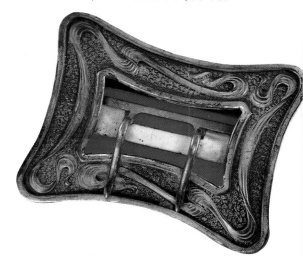

Buckle, unmarked, c. 1890. Rectangle shaped, imitation double prong closure, cast silver on brass, 3.25" x 2.5". $50-60.

Clasp, unmarked, 1910. Grapes, vines, and leaves, oxidized stamped brass, 3" x 2". $20-30.

Clasp, unmarked, c. 1890. Plated wings, cast leaves on stem with faceted cut steels at the tips, ball and chain at center, 6.5" x 1.25". $40-50.

Buckle, marked "Sterling front," c. 1900. Rectangular shaped, stamped decorative pattern, double prong closure, 3" x 2.5". $75-100.

Clasp, marked "Germany," c. 1920. Rectangle, oxidized stamped brass, flower design, 2.75" x .75". $10-20.

Clasp, unmarked, c. 1890. Shield design, oxidized stamped brass iris on stem, center cover plate with flower design, 2.75" x 2.5". $35-45.

Buckle, unmarked, c. 1900. Square shaped, oxidized stamped brass with three imitation prong set amethyst colored glass, 2.25" x 2.25". $15-25.

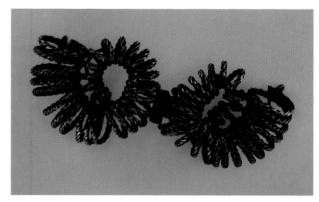

Clasp, unmarked, c. 1925. Tapered spirals of oxidized rope steel, 3.5" x 1.5". $15-25.

Buckle, unmarked, c. 1910. Rectangle shaped, silver on brass decorative design, 3" x 1.5". $30-50.

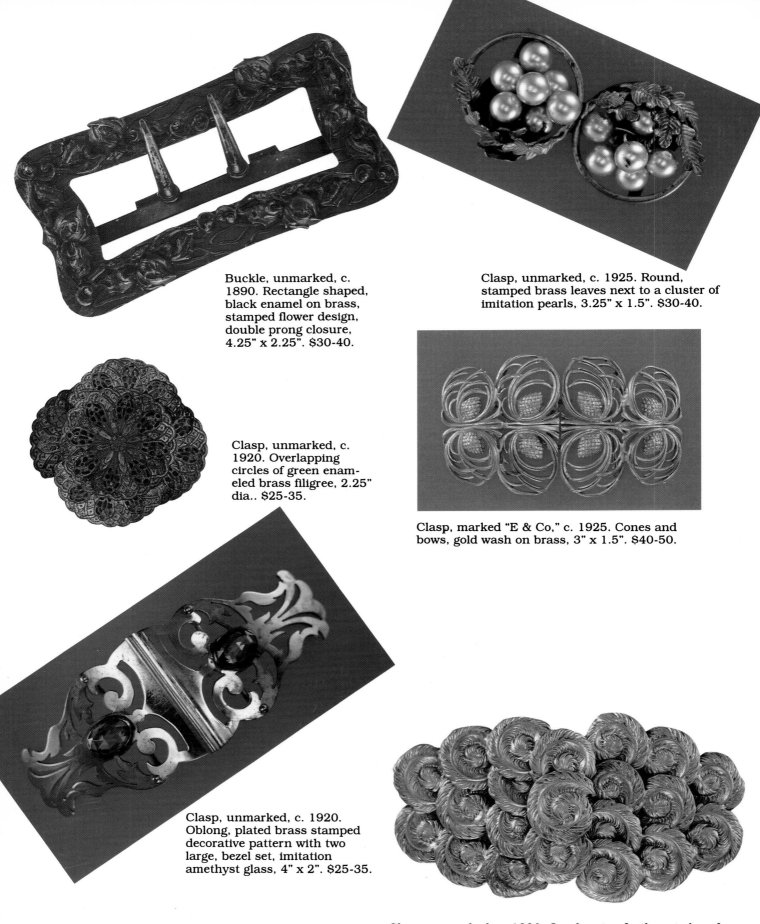

Buckle, unmarked, c. 1890. Rectangle shaped, black enamel on brass, stamped flower design, double prong closure, 4.25" x 2.25". $30-40.

Clasp, unmarked, c. 1925. Round, stamped brass leaves next to a cluster of imitation pearls, 3.25" x 1.5". $30-40.

Clasp, unmarked, c. 1920. Overlapping circles of green enameled brass filigree, 2.25" dia.. $25-35.

Clasp, marked "E & Co," c. 1925. Cones and bows, gold wash on brass, 3" x 1.5". $40-50.

Clasp, unmarked, c. 1920. Oblong, plated brass stamped decorative pattern with two large, bezel set, imitation amethyst glass, 4" x 2". $25-35.

Clasp, unmarked, c. 1920. Overlapping feather circles of gold washed stamped brass, 4.25" x 2.25". $35-45.

Clasp, unmarked, c. 1900. Stamped brass head of woman, mounted on a brass filigree background, 3.75" x 1.75". $40-50.

Clasp, unmarked, c. 1910. Brass ivy with berries mounted on a tinted oxidized disc, 4.25" x 2". $45-55.

Buckle, unmarked, c. 1900. Scroll pattern of oxidized stamped brass with two heart shaped, blue pressed glass stones, and one oblong prong set glass stone, 2.5" x 2". $30-40.

Clasp, unmarked, c. 1910. Frog on lily pad with flower, gold washed stamped brass, 3.25" x 2.75". $35-50.

Clasp, unmarked, c. 1900. Shield shaped oxidized brass with ornamental brass pieces mounted to shield, 2" x 2.25". $30-40.

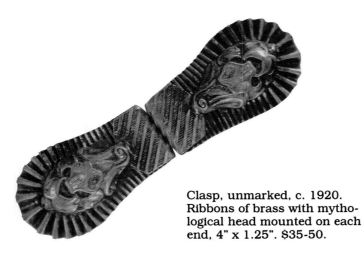

Clasp, unmarked, c. 1920. Ribbons of brass with mytho-logical head mounted on each end, 4" x 1.25". $35-50.

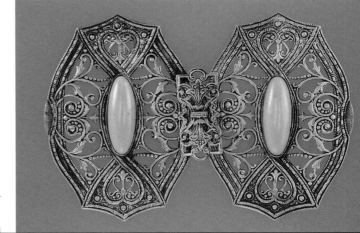

Clasp, unmarked, c. 1900. Oblong, gold washed stamped filigree bezel set, pressed glass, imitation coral centered on each half, 4" x 2.5". $35-45.

Clasp, unmarked, c. 1920. Round, black trim on brass filigree, orange pressed glass flower centers bezel set, 3.25" x 1.5". $30-40.

Clasp, unmarked, c. 1920. Oblong, gold washed stamped brass flower pattern, prong set imitation ruby centered on clasp, 3" x 1.75". $30-40.

Clasp, unmarked, c. 1925. Three gold washed stamped brass maple leaves, 4" x 2". $40-50.

Clasp, unmarked, c. 1910. Scalloped circles of gold wash brass filigree with bezel set, imitation turquoise stones, 4.5" x 2.25". $40-50.

Clasp, unmarked, c. 1920. Circles of stamped brass filigree, with brass balls mounted in the centers, 3.75" x 1.75". $35-45.

Clasp, unmarked, c. 1925. Overlapping leaves, gold wash brass with two brass flowers at center, 4" x 2.5". $35-45.

Clasp, unmarked, c. 1930. Round circles of brass with seaweed leaves and a shell base, 3.5" x 1.75". $30-40.

Clasp, marked "Germany," c. 1910. Octagonal, German nickel stamped brass with flower, 3" x 1.25". $15-20.

Buckle, marked "D.R.G.M. N:425672," c. 1925. Square with rounded corners, flower pattern, silver on brass, 2.25" x 2.5". $50-60.

Clasp, unmarked, c. 1890. Silver on brass, hand etched design, 3" x 1.75". $40-50.

Clasp, marked "B3057 FN&Co," c. 1910. Circles of leaves around a cherubim, black oxide on silver base, 2.5" x 1.25". $100-125.

Buckle, unmarked, c. 1880. Rectangle shaped, four prong closure, etched pattern on German nickel plated steel, 3.25" x 1.25". $30-40.

Buckle, marked "Sterling," c. 1905. Square shape with fancy trimmed edge sterling on brass, 2" x 1.75". $30-40.

Clasp, unmarked, c. 1900. Three joined circles with six leaves overlapping, stamped oxidized metal, ball and chain trim, 3.5" x 1.75". $35-40.

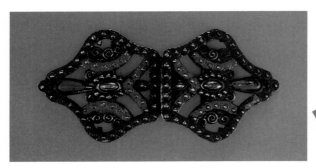

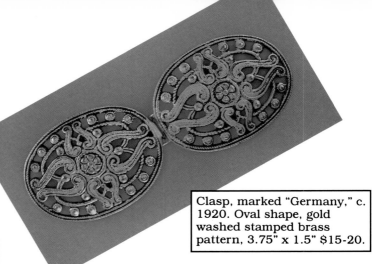

Clasp, marked "Germany," c. 1900. Five sided stamped pattern with green enamel trim, oxidized metal, 3" x 1.5". $15-20.

Clasp, marked "Germany," c. 1920. Oval shape, gold washed stamped brass pattern, 3.75" x 1.5" $15-20.

Clasp, marked "Czechoslova-kia," c. 1900. Oval shaped, gold washed brass filigree, diamond pattern, 2.5" x 1.5". $20-30.

Clasp, marked "Germany," c. 1900. Oval shaped, stamped circle of flowers with green enamel trim on brass, 1.75" x 1.5". $15-20.

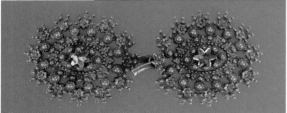

Clasp, unmarked, c. 1900. Knobby ovals of stamped brass with a star shaped faceted cut steel riveted to the center, 3" x 1.25". $20-25.

Clasp, unmarked, c. 1900. CHERUB ON A SEAHORSE, cast figure on a plated metal back, 4" x 1.25". $35-50.

Clasp, unmarked, c. 1900. PENSIVE CHERUB, stamped metal with enamel painted figure, 4" x 2". $30-35.

Clasp, unmarked, c. 1925. Circular hammered brass, head with turban, 3" x 1.5". $25-35.

Clasp, unmarked, c. 1900-1918. JUPITER AND MINERVA, stamped and tinted brass, 4.5" x 1.5". $50-75.

Clasp, unmarked, c. 1850-1900. ITALIAN VILLA. Stamped and tinted brass in a double border; an outer border of pierced brass with heart motif and an inner border with raised edge, 3.25" x 1.5". $30-40.

Clasp, unmarked, c. 1890-1900. CLEOPATRA AND THE ASP from Shakespeare's Anthony and Cleopatra. Stamped and tinted brass with a shiny liner under the rim, steel back, 3.25" x 1.5". $30-40.

Clasp, unmarked, c. 1900. FLOWERS **ON** WOOD. Tinted brass flowers on **wood** back in metal rim with Japanned metal back plate, ball and chain trim, 3.75" x 1.5". $30-40.

Clasp, unmarked, c. 1880-1900. PIERROT AND PIERRETTE, characters in French pantomime. Stamped brass figures applied to a textured brass cup with a flat mirrored white metal crescent moon applied under the rim, 3.5" x 1.5". $25-35.

Clasp, unmarked, c. 1850-1900. HECTOR, son of Priam, King of Troy, stamped brass applied to dark painted brass liner with brass stamped rim, 3" x 1.5". $30-40.

Clasp, unmarked, c. 1900. IVY LEAVES ON A FENCE. A stamped brass design decorated with a cut steel on a metal back, 2.25" x 1". $30-40.

Clasp, unmarked, c. 1900. ROSE within a leaf border. Cast base metal on a brass rimmed base, 3.25" x 1.5". $35-40.

Clasp, unmarked, c. 1900. CARNATIONS. Silvered brass with metal back, 2.5" x 1.25". $20-30.

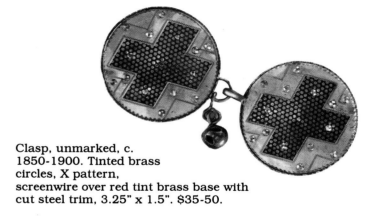

Clasp, unmarked, c. 1900. LILIES OF THE VALLEY. Tinted stamped brass flowers with cut steel trim on a textured brass base, 2.5" x 1.25". $30-40.

Clasp, unmarked, c. 1900. BIRD IN FLIGHT, HOLDING BRANCH IN BEAK. Stamped tinted brass on wood background with brass rimmed base, 3.5" x 1.5". $40-60.

Clasp, unmarked, c. 1850-1900. Tinted brass circles, X pattern, screenwire over red tint brass base with cut steel trim, 3.25" x 1.5". $35-50.

Clasp, unmarked, c. 1890. CHRYSANTHE-MUM. Stamped and tinted brass with white metal collet, 2.5" x 1". $20-30.

Clasp, unmarked, c. 1890. SPIKE. Metal spike on imitation brass wood back with metal rimmed back plate, 3.25" x 1.5". $30-40.

Clasp, unmarked, c. 1900. COTTON PLANT. Stamped pierced brass over a dark tinted brass background with a shiny white liner under the rim, 2.75" x 1.25". $30-40.

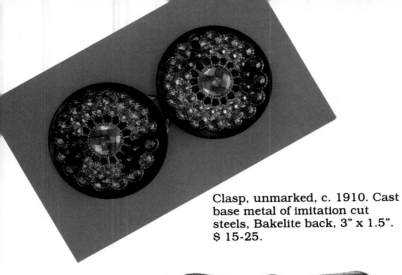

Clasp, unmarked, c. 1910. Cast base metal of imitation cut steels, Bakelite back, 3" x 1.5". $ 15-25.

Buckle, unmarked, c. 1900. Oval shaped silver on brass with Peacock pairs on top and bottom, imitation closure, 2.5" x 2". $35-50.

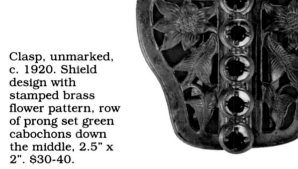

Clasp, unmarked, c. 1920. Shield design with stamped brass flower pattern, row of prong set green cabochons down the middle, 2.5" x 2". $30-40.

Clasp, unmarked, c. 1910. Art Nouveau, gold wash stamped brass head of woman with flowing hair, 4" x 2.25". $50-75.

Buckle, unmarked, c. 1940. Easel shaped, etched flower pattern in brass with copper center piece, 4" x 3.5". $30-40.

Clasp, unmarked, c. 1900. DAISIES. Pewter over a painted metal background with brass collet, steel back, 3" x 1.5". $30-40.

Clasp, unmarked, c. 1900. IVY. Stamped brass pattern of vine and ivy leaves, 3.25" x 1.5". $25-35.

Clasp, unmarked, c. 1900. FOUR BIRDS ON A BRANCH. A stamped pewter design mounted on a pierced white metal background with a mirrored metal liner underneath, 2.75" x 1.25". $30-40.

Clasp, unmarked, c. 1900. BIRD ON A BRANCH. Pewter over textured brass base, shiny white liner under a brass rim, 3.5" x 1.5". $30-40.

Clasp, marked "Depose," c. 1910. Russian style, quarter moon around heads of a turbaned man and a veiled woman, detailed sword fastens clasp together, stamped brass, 3.5" x 2.5". $100-125.

Buckle, adornment, marked "Patd May 16.05," c. 1905. Oblong, ribboned pattern, three bezel set rhinestones and a large green bezel set slag stone centered, with large safety pin attached to back mount. Safety pin attached to inside of skirt or petticoat and hooked over belt or sash, 2.75" x 3". $50-75.

Clasp, unmarked, c. 1900. Stamped oxidized metal, imitation closures, patterned center pieces attached to end pieces with chain, 4.5" x 2". $25-35.

Clasp, unmarked, c. 1900. LION IN CAGE, stamped brass base trimmed in faceted cut steels, 3" x 1.5". $50-75.

Clasp, unmarked, c. 1900. Carnation bouquet, stamped brass on plated base fastened with faceted cut steel, 2.5" x 1". $20-25.

Clasp, unmarked, c. 1850-1900. Wood backed, stamped brass flowers mounted to a plated base by faceted cut steels, 3.25" x 1.5". $40-60.

Clasp, unmarked, c. 1925. Triangle shaped, oxidized cast base metal, flowers and berries with prong set multi-colored glass stones, 3.5" x 1.75". $35-40.

Clasp, unmarked, c. 1900. DRAGON SLAYER, stamped brass, warrior on horse fighting dragon, 3.5" x 1.5". $35-40.

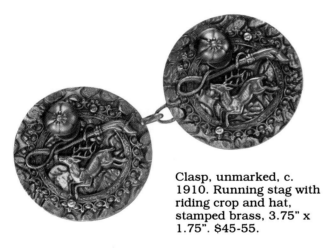

Clasp, unmarked, c. 1910. Running stag with riding crop and hat, stamped brass, 3.75" x 1.75". $45-55.

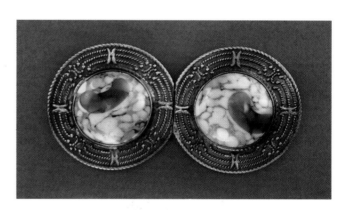

Clasp, marked, c. 1910. Round, die cut base with bezel set polished agate stones, centered, 3" x 1.5". $35-40.

Clasp, unmarked, c. 1935. Arrow feather design, metal base with bezel set blue cabochons, centered, 5.25" x 2". $25-35.

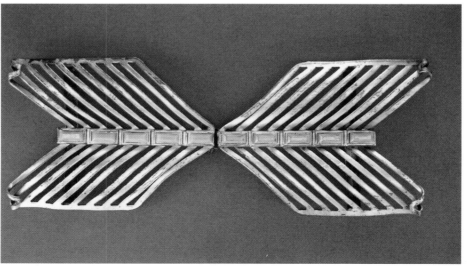

Clasp, unmarked, c. 1900. Round, polished base with stamped brass basket of flowers, 2.75" x 1.25". $30-40.

Clasp, unmarked, c. 1920. Brass circles of grape leaves and grapes of black beads, all wired to a brass perforated base, 3.25" x 1.5". $35-45.

Clasp, unmarked, c. 1930. Patterned brass base, high relief trim along two thirds of base, three bezel set paste, 3.5" x 1.75". $35-40.

Clasp, unmarked, c. 1900. Scalloped plated brass base, cast oxidized brass sailing ship with the word PURITAN, 3.75" x 1.75". $50-60.

Clasp, unmarked, c. 1890. MARY STUART, two piece stamped base metal in high relief on plated brass, base plate, 3.5" x 1.75". $35-45.

Clasp, unmarked, c. 1920. Round stamped brass, open work pattern with pink, green, and red bezel set stones, 4" x 1.75". $35-40.

Clasp, unmarked, c. 1930. Stamped rose pattern, high relief, plated, 3.25" x 1". $25-35.

Clasp, marked "Germany," c. 1930. Rectangle shape, stamped brass flower pattern with blue and brown enamel, 2.75" x 1.25". $30-35.

Clasp, unmarked, c. 1920. Studded shields in a branch frame with foliage, oxidized stamped brass, 3.75" x 1.25". $30-35.

Clasp, marked "Made in Czechoslovakia," c. 1900. Rectangles of tan pressed glass surrounded by brass filigree, 3" x 1.5". $40-50.

Clasp, unmarked, c. 1920. Stamped brass grapes and leaves on a textured plated brass base, 3" x 1.25". $30-35.

Clasp, unmarked, c. 1920. Circles of stamped brass overlapping leaves, 3" x 1.5". $35-45.

Clasp, unmarked, c. 1930. Two leaf flower with rhinestone center, leaf shape filigree base of oxidized stamped metal, 2.5" x 1". $30-35.

Clasp, unmarked, c. 1910. Stamped brass circles of blackberries and leaves, 3" x 1.25". $35-40.

Clasp, marked "Made in Czechoslovakia, E.S. Geschutzt," c. 1920. Six sided stamped brass, horse shoe pattern on filigree on a metal backplate, 1.25" x 1.25". $25-30.

Clasp, marked "Made in Germany," c. 1920. Oblong shape, stamped brass pattern foil under glass center piece, 2.75" x 1.25". $30-40.

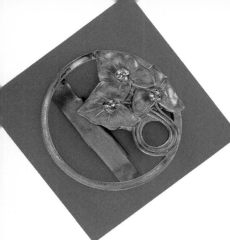

Buckle, unmarked, c. 1930. Ivy leaves with prong set rhinestones, gold wash on a stamped brass base, 1.75" dia. $20-25.

Buckle, unmarked, c. 1925. Curls of flowers and leaves, gold washed brass base circle with imitation closure, 2" dia. $20-25.

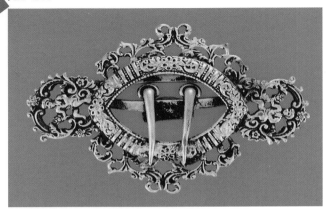

Buckle, unmarked, c. 1910. Oblong shaped, Cherubims on each end with fancy trim, double imitation closure, 3.5" x 2". $25-30.

Clasp, unmarked, c. 1920. Seven sided oxidized stamped metal, flower pattern, 4" x 1.25". $30-40.

Clasp, unmarked, c. 1890. Heart shaped, simple stamped flower design, 3.25" x 2". $20-25.

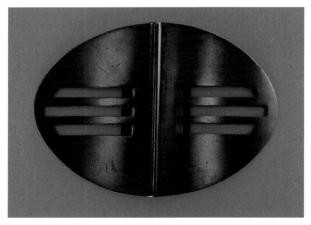

Clasp, marked "44," c. 1940. Oval shaped, rectangle slots in black oxidized stamped metal plate, 3" x 2.25". $10-20.

Clasp, unmarked, c. 1890. Shield pattern with tiny rose buds and leaves in a diamond pattern surrounding a vase with feathers, black enamel, 2.25" x 2.5". $25-30.

Buckle,Slide, marked, "Hecho en Mexico.F:925:,"c. 1930. Two half moon shaped plates riveted together, silver on brass, 3" x 2.5". $50-75.

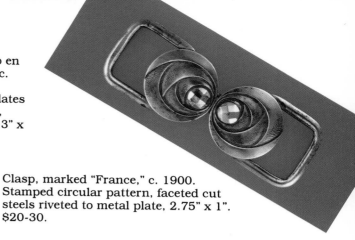

Clasp, marked "France," c. 1900. Stamped circular pattern, faceted cut steels riveted to metal plate, 2.75" x 1". $20-30.

Clasp, unmarked, c. 1920. Large flowers with flowing leaves in rope oval, gold washed brass, 4" x 1.5". $35-40.

Clasp, unmarked, c. 1900. Lily with green bezel set stoned stamen tips, stamped brass, 3.25" x 2.75". $35-40.

Clasp, unmarked, c. 1890. Oval shaped, oxidized, stamped brass pattern, 2.75" x 2.5". $35-40.

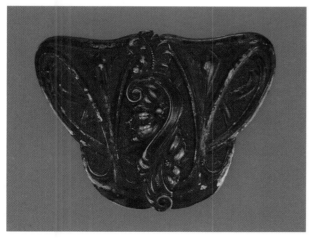

Clasp, unmarked, c. 1890. Shield design, flower and feather center piece, black enamel on stamped brass, 3" x 2.25". $30-40.

Clasp, unmarked, c. 1900. Two large flowers with flower and leaves centered, black enamel over stamped brass, 2.75" x 2.25". $35-40.

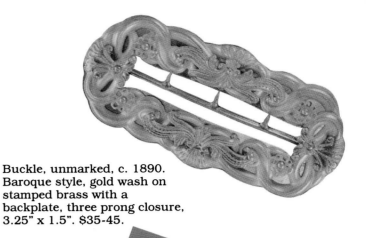

Buckle, unmarked, c. 1930. Inner and outer rectangle frames, flowers and leaves pattern in between, single closure, stamped brass flowers, metal base, 3.5" x 2.25". $25-35.

Buckle, unmarked, c. 1890. Baroque style, gold wash on stamped brass with a backplate, three prong closure, 3.25" x 1.5". $35-45.

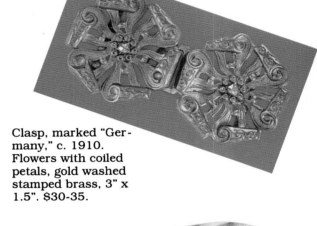

Buckle, unmarked, c. 1890. Rectangle shaped flower and leaf motif with fancy bows on each side, single closure, gold wash stamped brass, 5.5" x 2". $30-35.

Clasp, marked "Germany," c. 1910. Flowers with coiled petals, gold washed stamped brass, 3" x 1.5". $30-35.

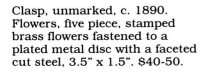

Buckle, unmarked, c. 1900. Oval shaped, gold washed stamped brass flowers on textured brass base, imitation closure, 2.5" x 1.75". $30-35.

Buckle, slide, unmarked, c. 1900. Oblong shaped, simple rope design with gold wash brass, 4.5" x 1.75". $20-25.

Clasp, unmarked, c. 1890. Flowers, five piece, stamped brass flowers fastened to a plated metal disc with a faceted cut steel, 3.5" x 1.5". $40-50.

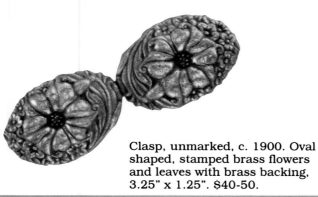

Clasp, unmarked, c. 1900. Oval shaped, stamped brass flowers and leaves with brass backing, 3.25" x 1.25". $40-50.

Clasp, unmarked, c. 1905. SARA BERNHARDT, as L'Aiglon, die stamped silver on metal, 3.5" x 1.5". $40-50.

Clasp, unmarked, c. 1890. Stamped brass circles of flowers, blue slag pressed glass stone, prong set with ribbons of brass, 5.25" x 2.5". $40-50. *Ulta Lowe collection.*

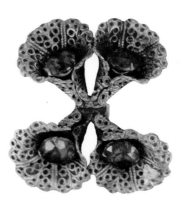

Clasp, marked "May 22.94," Coiled dragons, oxidized stamped brass, ring fasteners, 5.5" x 2". $50-75. *Ulta Lowe collection.*

Clasp, unmarked, c. 1900. Women's heads, baroque style trim with oxidized stamped brass, 3.5" x 2". $40-50. *Ulta Lowe collection.*

Clasp, unmarked, c. 1920. Morning Glory shape, stamped brass, patterned with prong set green stones in the centers, 2.25" x 2". $35-40. *Ulta Lowe collection.*

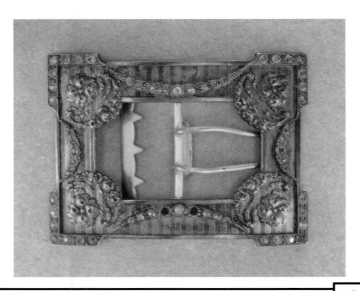

Buckle, unmarked, c. 1880. Rectangle shaped, die stamped flower pattern with pavé set rose and red colored stones following flower design, double prong closure, 3.25" x 2.5". $40-50. *Ulta Lowe collection.*

Buckle, unmarked, c. 1910. Oval shaped, stamped decorative trim on metal base, imitation closure, 3.25" x 2.5". $35-40. *Ulta Lowe collection.*

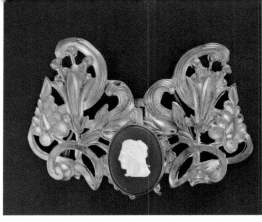

Clasp, unmarked, c. 1900. Gold washed, stamped brass pattern of flowers and leaves, bezel set glass oval with glass cameo, 3" x 2". $35-40.

Cape clasp, unmarked, c. 1920. Stamped brass shell design circles on triangle base, brass backplate joined by two brass rings and a link, 5.5" x 2". $35-45.

Cape clasp, unmarked, c. 1930. Oxidized, cast base metal with high relief filigree, with prong set faceted emerald colored stone centered, joined by fancy connecting link, 5" x 1.75". $40-45.

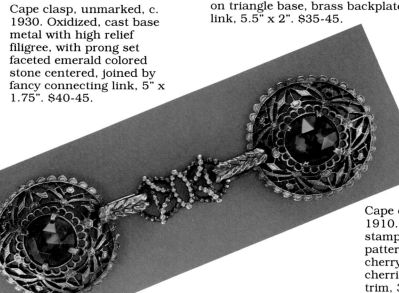

Cape clasp, unmarked, c. 1910. German nickel on stamped brass, shell pattern with sprigs of cherry tree, leaves, and cherries, ball and chain trim, 3.5" x 1.5". $30-35.

Cape clasp, unmarked, c. 1900. Stamped brass ovals with Victorian style trim, joined by single brass rope ring, 4.75" x 1.5". $25-30.

Cape clasp, unmarked, c.
1930. Oxidized stamped brass
leaves joined by a brass rope
ring, 4" x 1.5". $20-25.

Cape clasp, unmarked, c. 1930.
Art Deco style, stamped brass
pattern joined by a brass chain
mesh, 6.25" x 1.25". $25-30.

Cape clasp, unmarked, c. 1930.
Petunia type flower design, plated
stamped brass, joined by a chain,
4.5" x 1.5". $25-30.

Cape clasp, unmarked, c.
1900. Oxidized ovals of
twisted brass filigree leaves
covering a red prong set
stone, 4" x 1.5". $40-50.

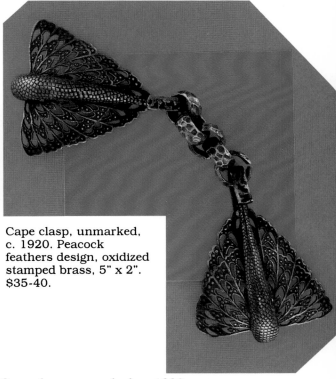

Cape clasp, unmarked,
c. 1920. Peacock
feathers design, oxidized
stamped brass, 5" x 2".
$35-40.

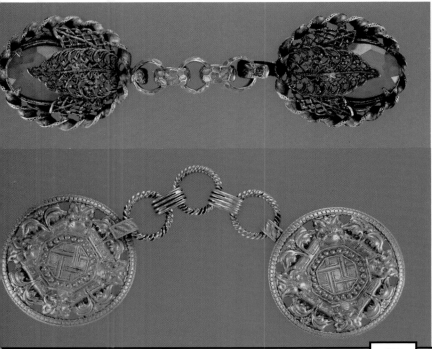

Cape clasp, unmarked, c. 1920.
Stamped brass circles with a rolled
edge, Victorian pattern, joined by brass
rope rings and two links, 6" x 1.75".
$25-30.

Cape clasp, unmarked, c. 1900. Stamped brass circles with brass rope edge, high relief, Victorian style, with green cabochons prong set at center, joined by four brass ribbon ovals, 6" x 1.75". $35-50.

Cape clasp, unmarked, c. 1900. Flower shaped, brass formed leaves with bezel set brown cabochons at center, joined by four oval shaped stamped pattern links, 6" x 1.75". $40-45.

Cape clasp, unmarked, c. 1910. Stamped brass rolled ribbed triangles, with brass three leave sprig on top, joined by two oblong brass rope links, 5.25" x 1.5". $35-40.

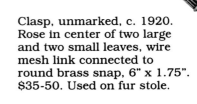

Clasp, unmarked, c. 1920. Rose in center of two large and two small leaves, wire mesh link connected to round brass snap, 6" x 1.75". $35-50. Used on fur stole.

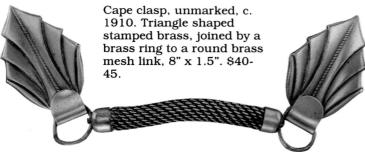

Cape clasp, unmarked, c. 1910. Triangle shaped stamped brass, joined by a brass ring to a round brass mesh link, 8" x 1.5". $40-45.

Clasp, unmarked, c. 1925. Egyptian revival, stamped brass winged horse and flower patterns, 3.5" x 2.25". $35-40.

Clasp, unmarked, c. 1930. Three clusters of feathers, high relief stamped copper, 3.75" x 2.5". $30-35.

Cape clasp, unmarked, c. 1920. Lion heads in high relief, silver on stamped brass joined by chain, 7" x 1.5". $35-45.

Cape clasp, unmarked, c. 1920. Lily pad leaves, German nickel on stamped metal joined by chain, 4.25" x 1.75". $25-35.

Cape clasp, unmarked, c. 1945. Stamped copper with small three leave pattern, joined by a single brass ring, 4.5" x 1.75". $20-25.

Clasp, unmarked, c. 1910. Mme. Chrysanthemum, one piece stamped brass, slightly convex with lattice trim, 3.5" x 1.75". $35-40.

Cape clasp, unmarked, c. 1925. Stamped brass dog heads mounted on Bakelite triangles, mounted on brass base, with two brass rope rings and a link, 5.75" x 1.75". $40-50.

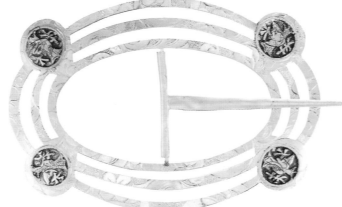

Buckle, unmarked, c. 1920. Stamped brass, flower pattern with different figures at each corner, single closure, 3.75" x 2.75". $30-35.

Cummerbund, marked, "Kandell & Marcus N.Y.," c. 1940. Chinaman, brass head surrounded by prong set etched glass in a cast base with Chinese characters and enameled flowers, five piece, chain linked, 5.5" x 2.75". $75-100.

Clasps, unmarked, c. 1930. Four different versions of Mme. Chrysanthemum, all stamped brass, *Left*: Flat stamped. *Top*: Silver on brass, convex. *Right*: Stamped, convex with rolled edge. *Bottom*: Stamped flat with filigree trim, 3" x 1.5". $30-45ea..

Cape clasp, unmarked, c. 1920. Blue prong set cabochon on layers of stamped brass petals mounted to a green Bakelite disc, joined by a figure eight loop, with a bezel mounted blue stone, 6.25" x 2". $50-60.

Cape clasp, unmarked, c. 1900. Stamped brass filigree in a fancy brass rope border with a pyramid shaped black Bakelite center, joined by two perforated brass rings and one link, 5" x 1.75". $50-60.

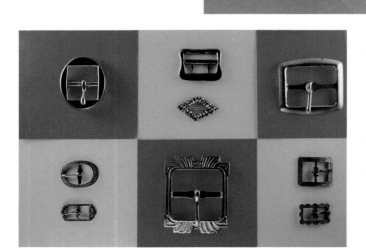

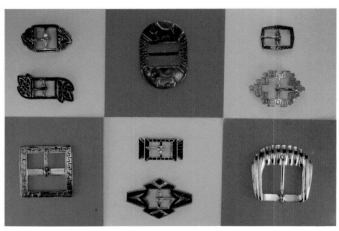

Misc. small buckles used on shoes, belts, and as ornaments. Size range of .5" to 2". $1-10ea..

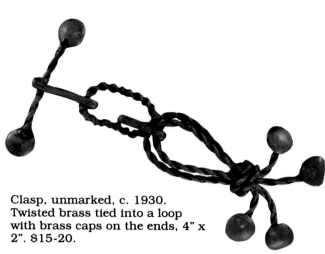

Cape clasp, unmarked, c. 1900. Cast base metal, twisted rope circles with filigree fans covering a prong set black pressed glass cabochon, joined by three stamped flower ovals, 6" x 1.75". $60-75.

Clasp, unmarked, c. 1930. Twisted brass tied into a loop with brass caps on the ends, 4" x 2". $15-20.

Cape clasp, unmarked, c. 1930. Silver on brass leaves joined by a stamped cupped chain, 5.75" x 1.5". $30-35.

Cape clasp, unmarked, c. 1910. Stamped brass bow on petal shaped base, and flowers on three point base joined by three stamped brass pattern oval links, 6.25" x 2". $45-50.

Clasp, unmarked, c. 1910. Oxidized stamped brass flowers and leaves riveted to a patterned copper base with hankerchief corners, with a faceted cut steel, 4.5" x 1.75". $45-50.

Cape clasp, unmarked, c. 1910. Oxidized stamped brass, curved feathers with a half round brass ball in curve, joined by two brass rings and a link, 5.5" x 1.75". $35-40.

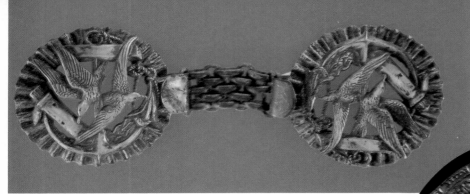

Cape clasp, unmarked, c. 1900. Oxidized stamped brass, gulls, anchor, and lighthouse in a rippled brass circle, joined by a brass mesh chain, 5.75" x 2". $50-75.

Clasp, unmarked, c. 1920. Egyptian revival, stamped brass Egyptian women on a brown Bakelite base, 4.25" x 2.75". $30-35.

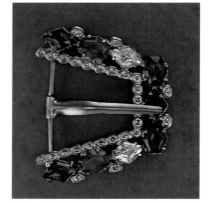

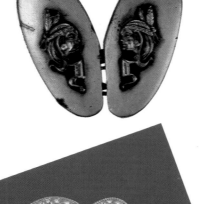

Clasp, marked, "C&R," c. 1830. Silver on brass stamped Indian princess heads, opposing views, 2" x 2". $50-75.

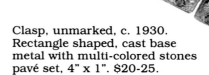

Clasp, unmarked, c. 1930. Rectangle shaped, cast base metal with multi-colored stones pavé set, 4" x 1". $20-25.

Clasp, unmarked, c. 1920. Patterned stamped brass with green, rose, and blue bezel set stones, 3.5" x 1.5". $30-35.

Buckle, unmarked, c. 1930. Gold washed cast base metal with prong set multi-colored stones, single closure prong, 2" x 2.75". $25-30.

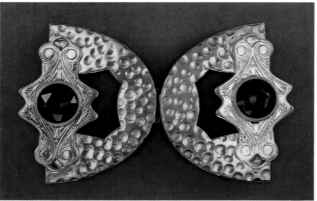

Clasp, unmarked, c. 1910. Half circles of gold washed hammered brass with bezel set green stones, centered, 3.5" x 2". $35-40.

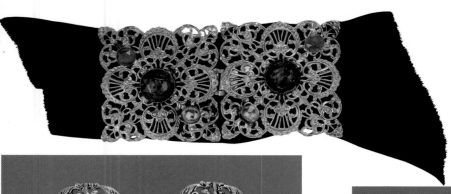

Clasp, unmarked, c. 1920. Rectangle shaped, shell pattern of gold washed stamped brass filigree, green, red, and amber bezel set stones,'on a black cloth, 3.5" x 2". $35-40.

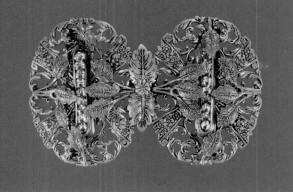

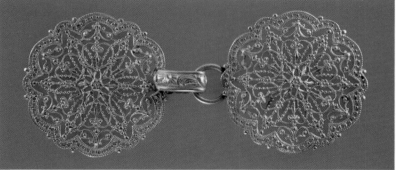

Clasp, unmarked, c. 1930. Oxidized stamped brass base, flower pattern with stamped brass leaves over a row of bezel set rhinestones, 3" x 2". $35-40.

Clasp, unmarked, c. 1920. Stamped brass filigree circles with scalloped edge, joined by hook and loop, 4.25" x 1.75". $20-25.

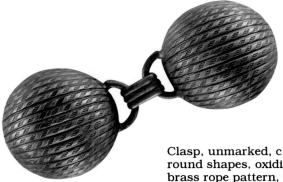

Clasp, unmarked, c. 1935. Half round shapes, oxidized stamped brass rope pattern, joined by a single link, 3.5" x 1.5". $25-30.

Clasp, unmarked, c. 1930. Heart shape, stamped brass pattern of flowers and stems, 3.75" x 1.75". $25-30.

Cummerbund, unmarked, c. 1930. Three piece, stamped brass base with brass leaves, decorated with red Bakelite roses, 6.25" x 1.75". $50-75.

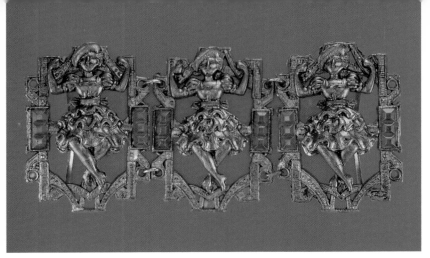

Cummerbund, unmarked, c. 1935. Cast, painted base metal, three dancing girls with red pressed glass trim, 4.5" x 2". $45-50.

Cummerbund, unmarked, c. 1935. Patterned stamped brass, overlapping leaves with amber colored plastic cabochons prong set in the center of each flower, 6.75" x 2.25". $40-45.

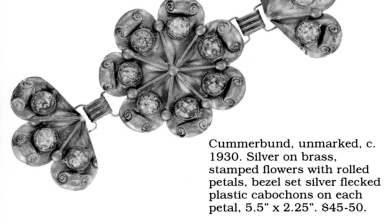

Cummerbund, unmarked, c. 1930. Silver on brass, stamped flowers with rolled petals, bezel set silver flecked plastic cabochons on each petal, 5.5" x 2.25". $45-50.

Cummerbund, unmarked, c. 1920. Stamped brass flowers with blue stones, paint silver, 6.25" x 2". $40-50.

Cummerbund, unmarked, c. 1920. Stamped oxidized brass base, flowers with green paste centers, 6.25" x 1.75". $40-50.

Cummerbund, unmarked, c. 1940. Oxidized stamped brass bubble edge circles, connected by four brass patterned links, 6.75" x 2.25". $35-45.

94

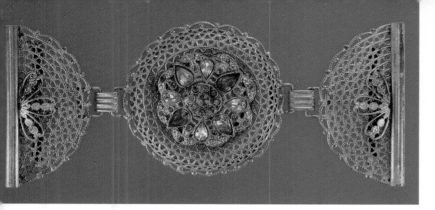

Cummerbund, unmarked, c. 1930. Stamped brass filigree circles and half circles, trimmed with green, blue, pink, and rose stones, joined by two links, 6.25" x 2.5". $45-55.

Cummerbund, unmarked, c. 1935. Gold wash on a brass base with cast base metal and imitation turquoise glass at center and on the ends, 5.25" x 1.25". $45-55.

Clasp, unmarked, c. 1935. Oxidized stamped brass leaves and squares, with six bezel set blue cabochons, 6.75" x 1.75". $45-55.

Cummerbund, unmarked, c. 1945. Stamped brass textured circles at each end with three button sized discs mounted to links, 6.25" x 1.5". $35-45.

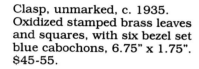

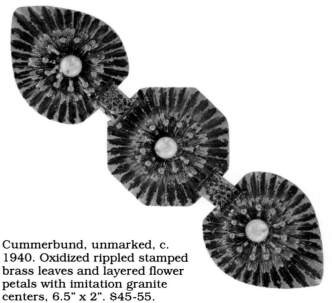

Cummerbund, unmarked, c. 1940. Oxidized rippled stamped brass leaves and layered flower petals with imitation granite centers, 6.5" x 2". $45-55.

Set, cummerbund, marked, "KIRSCHENBAUM PAT.PEND.N.Y.," c. 1935. Overlapping flower petals mounted on a brass base with rows of linked half rounds, 7.5" x 2". Two sew-on belt adornments of three rows of stamped brass half rounds, 1.25" x 2". $50-65.

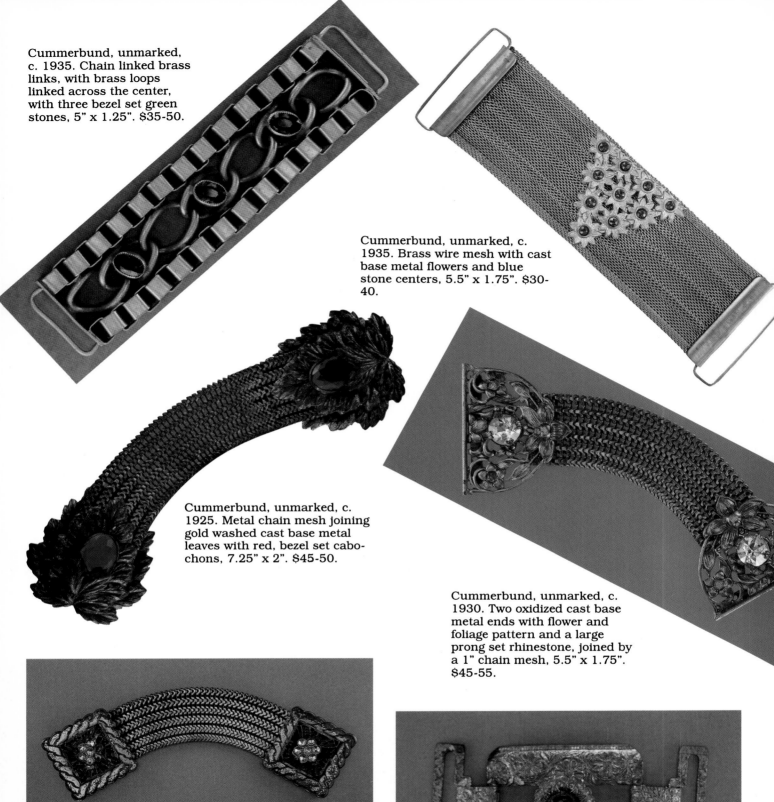

Cummerbund, unmarked, c. 1935. Chain linked brass links, with brass loops linked across the center, with three bezel set green stones, 5" x 1.25". $35-50.

Cummerbund, unmarked, c. 1935. Brass wire mesh with cast base metal flowers and blue stone centers, 5.5" x 1.75". $30-40.

Cummerbund, unmarked, c. 1925. Metal chain mesh joining gold washed cast base metal leaves with red, bezel set cabochons, 7.25" x 2". $45-50.

Cummerbund, unmarked, c. 1930. Two oxidized cast base metal ends with flower and foliage pattern and a large prong set rhinestone, joined by a 1" chain mesh, 5.5" x 1.75". $45-55.

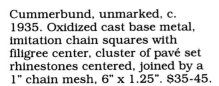

Cummerbund, unmarked, c. 1935. Oxidized cast base metal, imitation chain squares with filigree center, cluster of pavé set rhinestones centered, joined by a 1" chain mesh, 6" x 1.25". $35-45.

Cummerbund, unmarked, c. 1935. Gold washed stamped brass, flower pattern with a stamped brass flower with a centered green cabochon, 3.25" x 1.5". $25-35.

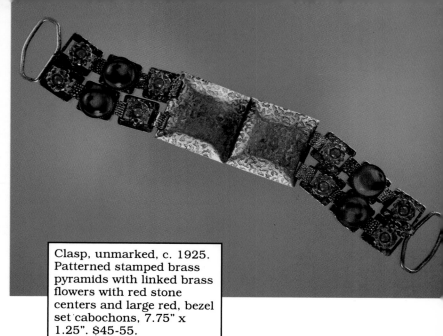

Cummerbund set, unmarked, c. 1950. Silver on brass stamped filigree ovals, with large blue prong set cabochons, joined by a link, 5" x 2". Matching pin, three cone shaped flowers, with blue paste in the heart of the flower, hung by loops, 2" x 3". $55-65.

Cummerbund, unmarked, c. 1935. Oxidized stamped brass filigree circle, with a large bezel set coral colored pressed glass cabochon, three rectangle links on each side, with small coral colored cabochons, 6.75" x 2.25". $45-55.

Cummerbund, unmarked, c. 1930. Three octagonal shaped stamped brass bases with stamped brass layers of leaves and flower petals, with bezel set imitation coral in the center, 5.75" x 1.75". $45-55.

Clasp, unmarked, c. 1920. Coiled white metal rings, folded triangles with mille-fiori glass cabochons, prong mounted, 5.25" x 1.5". $50-75. *Evelyn Gibbons collection.*

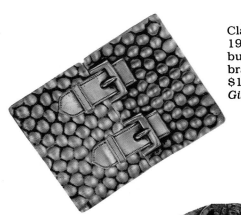

Clasp, unmarked, c. 1945. Buckle on a buckle, stamped brass, 2.25" x 1.75". $15-25. *Evelyn Gibbons collection.*

Clasp, unmarked, c. 1920. Silver on brass stamped pattern, Egyptian head, 3.5" x 2.25". $40-60. *Evelyn Gibbons collection.*

Clasp, unmarked, c. 1920. Oxidized stamped brass, foliage pattern, large scarab with an amber colored glass stone body, 3" x 2.5". $50-75. *Annie Frazier collection.*

Buckle, marked, "AK Depose," c. 1900. Stamped and etched brass rooster, 2.25" x 2.75". $50-75. *Annie Frazier collection.*

Rear view of moth buckle.

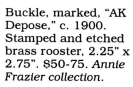

Buckle, unmarked, c. 1940. Cast brass moths facing each other, reverse side, etched fern leaves in a Japanned back, 3.75" x 2.5". $50-75. *Annie Frazier collection.*

Clasp, unmarked, c. 1900. Three hounds tied to a branch, cast brass figure on a metal disc, made from buttons, 2.75" x 1.25". $40-60.

Clasp, unmarked, c. 1910. PERRY AT THE POLE. Gold washed stamped brass scene of Admiral Perry at the pole, 4"x 2.5". $50-75. *Annie Frazier collection.*

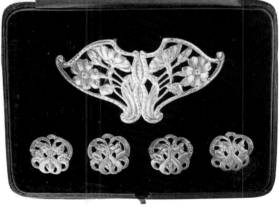

Clasp, unmarked, c. 1940. Silver on brass, flower pattern, stamped backplate with raised center flower, 3.25" x 2.5". $50-60.

Clasp, button set, box marked, "W&W Logan, Buchanan SI, Diamond Merchants, Goldsmiths & Silversmiths," c. 1900. Clasp marked, "#1479 M," buttons marked, "3,". Silver, flowers and foliage pattern. Box is 9" x 4.5". Clasp is 3.5" x 2.25". Buttons are 1" dia.. $500-800. *Annie Frazier collection.*

Buckle, unmarked, c. 1900. Oval shaped, gold washed, pierced backplate with brass flies and beetles, double prong closure, 3.25" x 2.5". $70-100.

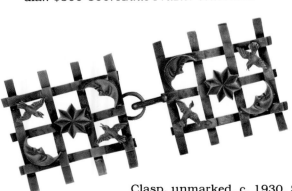

Clasp, unmarked, c. 1930. Square shape, brass lattice work with birds and moon faces, 3.5" x 1.5". $35-50.

Buckle, unmarked, c. 1890. Stamped brass with raised flowers pattern, brass extension with safety pin, (used to hold up petticoats), 3" x 2". $40-65.

Reverse view

Clasp, unmarked, c. 1900. Overlapping stamped brass leaves on the stem of a brass flower, front view, 4.75" x 1.5". $40-60.

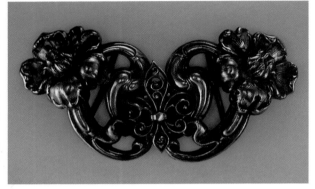

Clasp, unmarked, c. 1900. Silver on brass, stamped flowers with a center mounted fleur-de-lis, 3.5" x 1.5". $35-50.

Clasp, unmarked, c. 1930. Oxidized stamped brass bulldog head, 3" x 1.25". $35-45. *Evelyn Gibbons collection.*

Buckle, unmarked, c. 1910. Gibson girl head, stamped brass in high relief, trimmed in rhinestones, mounted to a brass plate, 3.5" x 2.75". $40-60. *Evelyn Gibbons collection.*

Buckle, unmarked, c. 1910. Victorian lady in bonnet, flowers and foliage on right and left, mounted on a brass ring, 6" x 3.75". $75-100. *Evelyn Gibbons collection.*

Clasp, unmarked, c. 1900. NIOBE, daughter of Tantalus, Greek mythology. Brass heads on a six sided German nickel plate, ball and chain trim, 3.75" x 2". $50-65. *Evelyn Gibbons collection.*

Clasp, unmarked, c. 1900. Gold washed brass, coiled snakes with flowers and foliage, 4" x 2.25". $50-65. *Evelyn Gibbons collection.*

Clasp, pin set, unmarked, c. 1930. Pirate head on a textured background, oxidized stamped brass, 3.5" x 2.5", pin is 2.5" x 2". $50-65. *Evelyn Gibbons collection.*

Belt, marked, "Solid Copper," c. 1955. Stamped copper belt, Indian designs with black enamel background. Overlapping panel on an elastic fabric, buckle is, 5.5" x 2". $75-85.

Belt, unmarked, c. 1930-1950. Hammered aluminim, padlock and crossed keys pattern panels joined by aluminum rings, 1.75" x 27". $50-65.

Belt, unmarked, c. 1950. Plated stamped brass panels joined by brass oval links, 1.5" x 26.5". $20-30.

Buckle, unmarked, c. 1910. Two Cherubims with roses and foliage, stamped brass, 5.5" x 2". $50-75.

Belt, unmarked, c. 1950. Plated stamped brass conchos joined by metal loops, Indian design, 1" x 25". $20-30.

Belt, unmarked, c. 1930-1950. Hammered aluminum panels with an etched design joined by hammered aluminum links, 1.5" x 25". $50-60.

Belt, unmarked, c. 1960. Cast white metal swans joined by metal loops, 3.25" x 30". $15-25.

Belt, unmarked, c. 1930-1950. Hammered aluminum squares with leaves and grapes design joined by hammered aluminum loops, 1.5" x 30". $50-75.

Belts, unmarked, c. 1955. Stamped copper butterflies, joined by copper rings, .75" x 31". Plated metal butterflies, joined by metal links, 1.25" x 32". $20-30 ea.

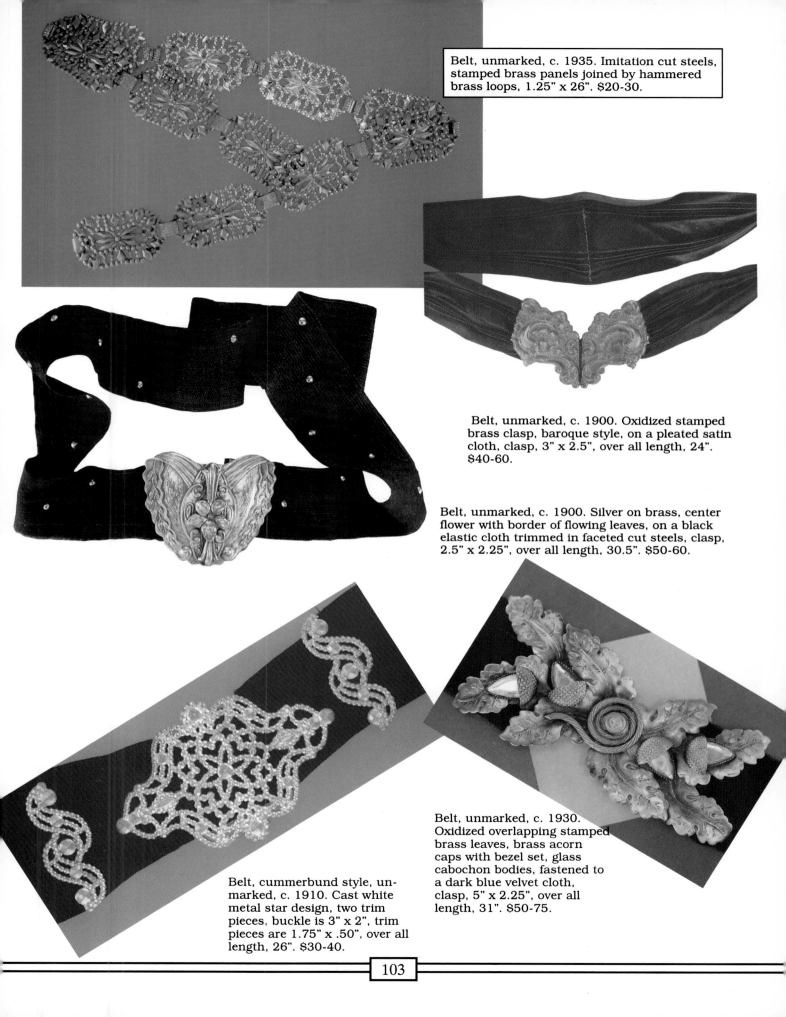

Belt, unmarked, c. 1935. Imitation cut steels, stamped brass panels joined by hammered brass loops, 1.25" x 26". $20-30.

Belt, unmarked, c. 1900. Oxidized stamped brass clasp, baroque style, on a pleated satin cloth, clasp, 3" x 2.5", over all length, 24". $40-60.

Belt, unmarked, c. 1900. Silver on brass, center flower with border of flowing leaves, on a black elastic cloth trimmed in faceted cut steels, clasp, 2.5" x 2.25", over all length, 30.5". $50-60.

Belt, cummerbund style, unmarked, c. 1910. Cast white metal star design, two trim pieces, buckle is 3" x 2", trim pieces are 1.75" x .50", over all length, 26". $30-40.

Belt, unmarked, c. 1930. Oxidized overlapping stamped brass leaves, brass acorn caps with bezel set, glass cabochon bodies, fastened to a dark blue velvet cloth, clasp, 5" x 2.25", over all length, 31". $50-75.

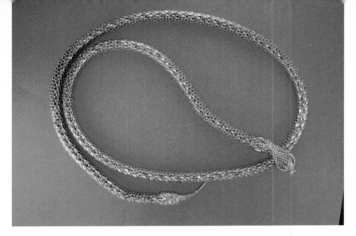

Belt, marked, "Made in Czechosolvakia," c. 1910. Stamped brass filigree, clasp with matching buttons, fastened to a red satin cloth, clasp, 2.75" x 1.5", buttons, 1.1" dia, over all length, 26.5". $35-50.

Belt, unmarked, c. 1955. Shape of snake, imitation scales, gold color, cast metal head with red glass eyes, head clamps to body as a fastener, over all length, 38". $50-60.

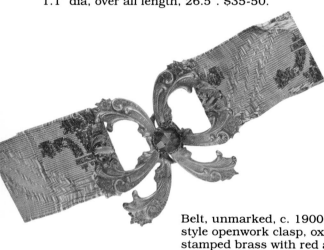

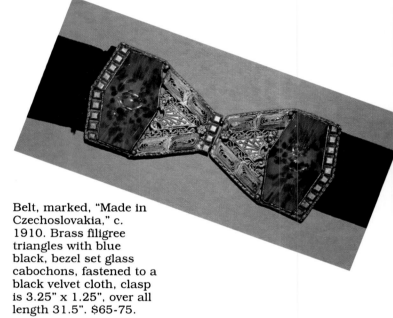

Belt, unmarked, c. 1900. Baroque style openwork clasp, oxidized stamped brass with red and green glass stones, fastened to a gold embossed patterned cloth, clasp is 2.5" x 2.25" over all length, 25". $75-85.

Belt, marked, "Made in Czechoslovakia," c. 1910. Brass filigree triangles with blue black, bezel set glass cabochons, fastened to a black velvet cloth, clasp is 3.25" x 1.25", over all length 31.5". $65-75.

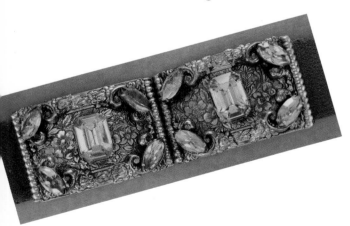

Belt, unmarked, c. 1935. Rectangle shaped clasp, cast brass with flower design, prong set amber colored glass stones, fastened to a red cloth, clasp is 4.25" x 1.5", over all length, 30". $60-75.

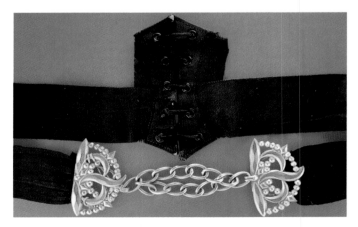

Belt, unmarked, c. 1905. Silver on brass imitation cut steels, half rounds joined by metal loops, fastened to a black cloth with an adjustment cinch on the back side, clasp is 6.5" x 2.25", over all length 26". $45-50.

Overall view

Belt, unmarked, c. 1900. Brass filigree clasp with prong set multi-colored stones, on a metal wrapped woven thread, with large and small multi-colored cabochons and brass triangles, clasp is 3" x 1.75", overall length, 32". $300-350.

Belt, unmarked, c. 1930. Stamped and formed brass base, center is shaped to mount a prong set amber colored glass stone. Two belt ornaments with stamped brass base mounts for a prong set glass stone, on brown satin cloth, buckle is 2"sq., ornaments are .75" x 1.5", over all length 29". $50-60.

Belt, unmarked, c. 1920. Oxidized stamped brass, grapes bordered by Lillies of the Valley, on a cord belt, 2.5" x 2", over all length 28". $40-50.

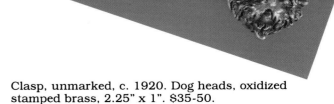

Belt, unmarked, c. 1920. Gold wash brass filigree base, with faceted bezel set glass stone at center, on blue velvet fabric, 3" x 2", over all length 26". $35-50.

Clasp, unmarked, c. 1920. Dog heads, oxidized stamped brass, 2.25" x 1". $35-50.

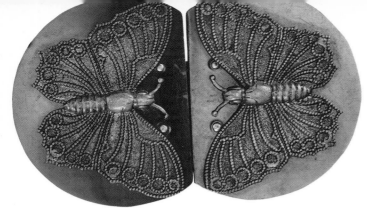

Buckle, marked "JW," c. 1910. Oval with four prong closure, unusual hinged fastener, 2" x 1.3". $20-30.

Clasp, unmarked, c. 1935. Butterflies, cast white base metal on a plastic base, 4.25" x 2.75". $35-50. *Louise Cook collection.*

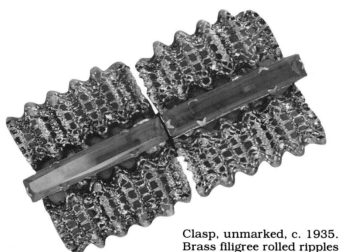

Clasp, unmarked, c. 1935. Brass filigree rolled ripples with prong set red glass bar down the center, 3.75" x 2". $40-50.

Clasp, unmarked, c. 1920. Oriental man and woman, white base metal on a silver on brass textured background, ball and chain trim, 3" x 2.25". $40-50.

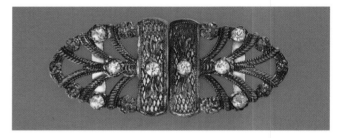

Clasp, unmarked, c. 1935. Oblong, flower and leaf design, prong set rhinestone trim, 2.8" x 1.25". $25-35.

Set, clasp and scarf slide, unmarked, c. 1910. Profile bust of Art Nouveau figures, silver on brass, 4" x 2.25", slide, 1" x 1.3". $75-100.

Cape clasp, unmarked, c. 1925. Stamped brass circles of flowers joined by two oval loops, 5.5" x 1.75". $35-50.

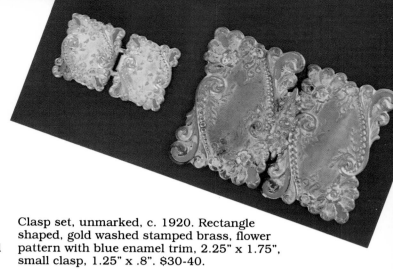

Cape clasp, unmarked, c. 1930. Stamped brass circle of loops with a filigree center and a prong set red faceted glass stone, centered, joined by a single large loop, 4.25" x 1.5". $35-50.

Clasp set, unmarked, c. 1920. Rectangle shaped, gold washed stamped brass, flower pattern with blue enamel trim, 2.25" x 1.75", small clasp, 1.25" x .8". $30-40.

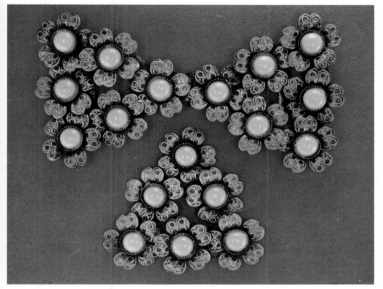

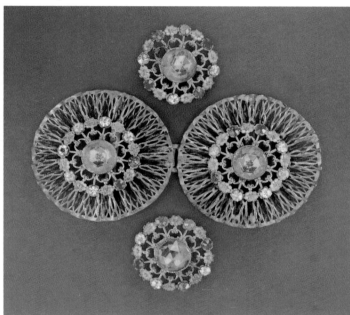

Buckle, clip set, unmarked, c. 1930. Triangles of six, five petaled stamped brass flowers with bezel set blue cabochon centers, 3.75" x 2", clip, 2" x 2" x 2". $40-50.

Clasp, button set, unmarked, c. 1920. Stamped brass rippled filigree circles, with a circle of prong set multi-colored stones, and a large bezel set amber stone at center, 4.5" x 2.25", button, 1.25" dia. $45-60.

Clasp, belt adornment set, unmarked, c. 1930. Baroque style silver on brass, with fleur-de-lis at center, two belt trim fleur-de-lises, clasp, 2.75" x 2.25", trims, 1.25" x 1.5". $35-50.

Cummerbund, unmarked, c. 1935. Gold washed stamped brass circle, with stamped brass flower petals and a blue pressed glass cabochon in the center, stamped brass chain links on each side, 6" x 2.5". $40-50.

Cummerbund, unmarked, c. 1945. Oxidized stamped brass squares, with bezel set green plastic centers, 5.5" x 1.75". $25-35.

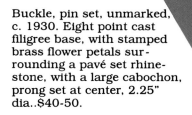

Buckle, pin set, unmarked, c. 1930. Eight point cast filigree base, with stamped brass flower petals sur-rounding a pavé set rhine-stone, with a large cabochon, prong set at center, 2.25" dia..$40-50.

Clasp,button set, unmarked, c. 1935. Gold washed stamped brass, sunburst with circle of colored prong set stones in the center, clasp, 3.25" x 1.75", button, 1" dia.. $35-45.

Clasp, slide set, unmarked, c. 1945. Silver on brass, stamped roses, 4" x 1.5". $25-30.

Clasp, dress clip set, unmarked, c. 1935. Oxidized stamped, and pierced brass cones with a circle of pavé set green stones, clasp 4" x 2", clip 2" dia.. $35-40.

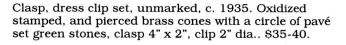

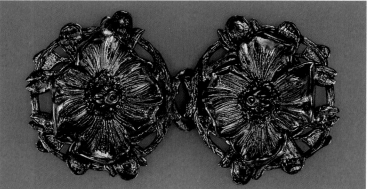

Clasp, unmarked, c. 1935. Silver on brass, stamped flowering dogwood in a vine and foliage ring, 3.75" x 2.25". $35-40.

Clasp, marked, "Made in Czechoslovakia,"c. 1930. Perforated stamped brass discs, red, blue, yellow, and orange colored flowers, 2.75" x 1.5". $25-35.

Clasp, unmarked, c. 1930. Oblong shaped, stamped brass rope pattern edge, with pansy and leaves, design, 5" x 1.5". $35-40.

Clasp, unmarked, c. 1935. Enameled, gold washed stamped brass, 'Persian Jewels' flower design, 4" x 1.75". $25-35.

Buckle, unmarked, c. 1910. Oxidized brass, crest shaped with baroque style heart in the center, 2.25" x 2". $20-30.

Clasp, unmarked, on card marked, "Foliage Ensemble Jewelry," c. 1950. Gold painted brass leaves, 4" x 2", card is 4.25" x 3.25". $15-25.

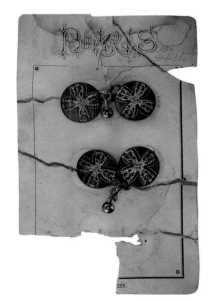

Clasp, unmarked, on card marked, "Paris," c. 1900. Round shaped, red oxidized discs with etched pattern, stamped brass pattern, cross shape fastened to top, ball and chain trim, 1" dia.. Card is 4.5" x 7". $35-50.

Clasp, button, salesman's sample card, marked "CARD 4026, Price Per Dozen, Trade Mark Registered, Beaver Brand, Thru Industry We Thrive, carded", c. 1930. Oxidized stamped brass leaves on a brass disc, various sizes of buttons and clasps in gold and silver. $60-75. *Clare Hatton collection.*

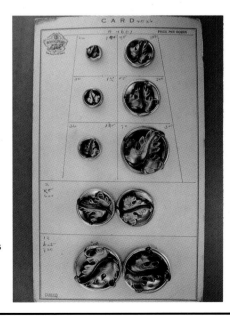

Clasp, marked, "C & R," c. 1920. Oblong shaped gilt on brass, flower and foliage pattern with oriental woman bust, 3.5" x 1.5". $75-100.

Clasp, marked, "Made in Indo China," c. 1930. Silver, different oriental scenes on each half, 3.75" x 1.75". $150-200.

Clasp, unmarked, c. 1900. Gold washed stamped brass, baroque styling, prong set faceted green glass jewel at center, unusual cloth fastener, cloth was crimped in a round bar then attached to the clasp by chain, 4" x 2". $40-65.

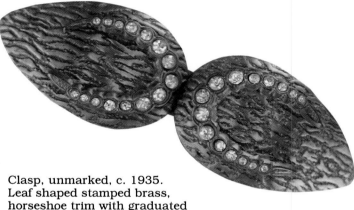

Clasp, unmarked, c. 1935. Leaf shaped stamped brass, horseshoe trim with graduated pavé set rhinestones, 4.75" x 1.75". $30-40.

Clasp, unmarked, c. 1930. Gold washed cast base metal, flower pattern with orange pressed glass roses, 2.75" x 2". $35-40.

Clasp, unmarked, c. 1900. LITTLE RED RIDING HOOD AND THE WOLF. Cast brass figures, mounted on plated discs, joined by a ball and chain, 3" x 1.5". $200-300. *Courtesy Mrs. Lula McCampbell.*

Clasp, unmarked, c. 1900. Stamped brass circles of rope trim with filigree flowers, and a faceted steel riveted to the center of the flower, 2.75" x 1.5". $35-50.

Belt, unmarked, c. 1900. Gold washed stamped brass filigree panels, joined by brass loops with prong set blue cabochon decorations, clasp is 3.5" x 2", over all length 24.5". $75-100.

Clasp, unmarked, c. 1890. Stamped brass flowers with faceted cut steels riveted to the flowers, attached to a plated steel plate, 3.5" x 1.5". $30-40.

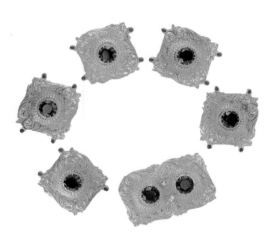

Belt pieces, unmarked, c. 1900. Gold washed, stamped brass buckle with decorative trim panels, each panel has an imitation amythyst prong set stone, two prong set rhinestones on the buckle, buckle is 2" x 1.25", panels are 1.25" x 1.5". $35-50.

Belt, unmarked, c. 1900. Gold washed stamped brass panels, flower design, alternating green stones and white enamel panels joined by brass links, buckle is 1.5" x 1.25", over all length 23.5". $75-100.

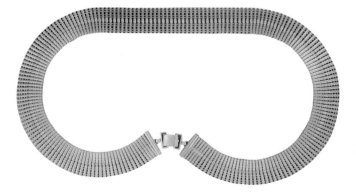

Belt, unmarked, c. 1900. Silver on brass, stamped open design panels joined by brass links, prong set green cabochon on buckle, green faceted prong set stones on each panel, buckle is 1.75"sq., over all length 27". $50-75.

Belt, unmarked, c. 1940. Brass rods connected by eight connecting links with snap link connector, over all length 26". $15-25.

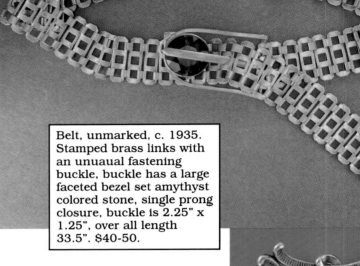

Belt, unmarked, c. 1890. Oxydized stamped brass, feather design with a large, clear, prong set faceted glass stone at center, clasp is 5" x 4", on a 4" wide elastic cloth, over all length 28.5". $75-100.

Belt, unmarked, c. 1935. Stamped brass links with an unuaual fastening buckle, buckle has a large faceted bezel set amythyst colored stone, single prong closure, buckle is 2.25" x 1.25", over all length 33.5". $40-50.

Buckle, unmarked, c. 1900. Cast brass oval shape, with two imitation closure prongs and Putti figures on each end, 3.5" x 2.25". $25-35.

Buckle, unmarked, c. 1900. Art Nouveau, silver on brass, woman with harp in a bell shape design surrounded by scroll work, 3.25" x 1.75". $75-100.

Clasp, unmarked, c. 1910. Champlevé enamel, green, black, and white, alligator down the center, surrounded by red flowers with green foliage and a blue and white border, in a cut to shape and pierced groundplate, 3.5" x 2.25". $75-100.

Clasp, unmarked, c. 1900. Tulip shape pattern and outline, cut to shape and pierced, gilt groundplate, champlevé enameling with faceted cut steels trim, blue, red, green, and yellow colors, 3.25" x 2". $100-125.

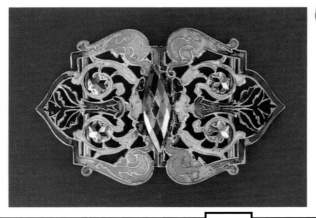

Clasp, marked "Metal Gilt," c. 1890. Pansies and foliage design in champlevé and basse-taille enameled shades of green, blue, and white on a cut to shape and pierced groundplate, 3.25" x 1.75". $150-200.

Clasp, marked "Metal Gilt," c. 1890. Cyclamen and foliage design in champlevé and basse-taille enameled shades of green, red, and pink on a cut to shape and pierced groundplate, 2.75" x 1.75". $150-200.

Clasp, marked, unreadable, c. 1900. Cloisonné butterfly, exquisite rare piece. Green, black, brown, gold, and silver colors in a gilt base, 3.25" x 2.25". $500-650.

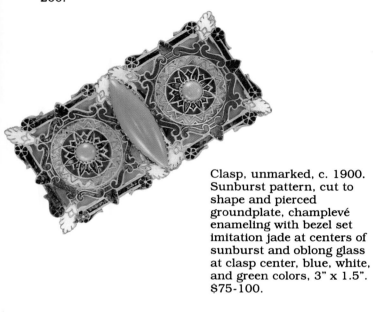

Clasp, unmarked, c. 1900. Sunburst pattern, cut to shape and pierced groundplate, champlevé enameling with bezel set imitation jade at centers of sunburst and oblong glass at clasp center, blue, white, and green colors, 3" x 1.5". $75-100.

Clasp, unmarked, c. 1900. Lattice work pattern, cut to shape and pierced, gilt groundplate, champlevé enameling with bezel set imitation amethyst stone at center, blue, white, red, violet, and green colors, 3.75" x 2.25". $75-100.

Clasp, unmarked, c. 1910. Overlapping circles with center crest, gold washed stamped brass with blue, white, and red enameling, 3" x 2". $40-60.

Clasp, unmarked, c. 1940. Ribbed leaf cut to shape, gilt ground-plate, champlevé enameling, royal blue color, 2.5" x 2.25". $40-50.

Buckle, unmarked, c. 1950. Brass, gold wash shield with mapleleaf crest of gold, green, and red enameled champlevé, 1.5" x 2". $20-30.

Clasp, marked "Made in Czechoslovakia IMIT," c. 1920. Flower design in champlevé and basse-taille enameled colors of orange, pink, blue, black, white, and green in a square groundplate, 2.25" x 1.5". $50-75.

Clasp, marked "Czechoslovakia," c. 1920. Gold, red, and violet roses with foliage, with violet, blue, and white background, cut to shape groundplate, design in champlevé and basse-taille enamel, 2.25" x 2". $100-125.

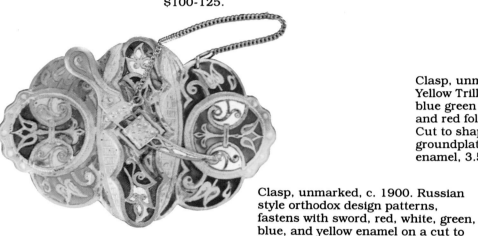

Clasp, unmarked, c. 1900. Yellow Trillium petals with a blue green background, green and red foliage, outlined in blue. Cut to shape champlevé groundplate, basse-taille enamel, 3.5" x 1.75". $100-150.

Clasp, unmarked, c. 1900. Russian style orthodox design patterns, fastens with sword, red, white, green, blue, and yellow enamel on a cut to shape groundplate, design in champlevé, 3.5" x 2.5". $125-150.

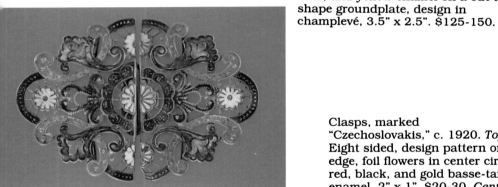

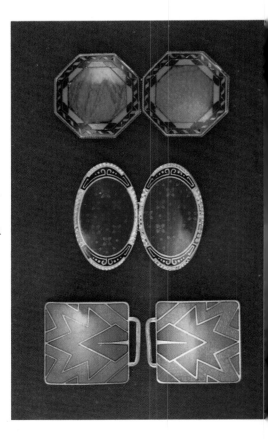

Clasps, marked "Czechoslovakis," c. 1920. *Top*: Eight sided, design pattern on edge, foil flowers in center circle, red, black, and gold basse-taille enamel, 2" x 1". $20-30. *Center*: Oval shape, foil flower pattern in royal blue basse-taille enamel, 1.75" x 1.5". $25-35. *Bottom*: Square geometric pattern, red and pink basse-taille enamel, 2.5" x 1". $20-25.

Clasp, unmarked, c. 1900. Flower pattern, stamped brass, blue, white, and red enamel, 3" x 2.25". $50-75.

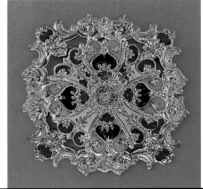

Buckle, unmarked, c. 1920. Squared stamped brass with scalloped edge, inner circle pattern of red flowers with blue, red, and green enamel trim, 2" x 2". $20-30.

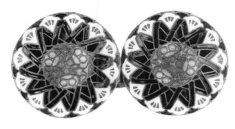

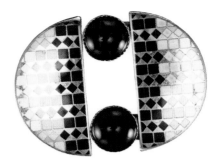

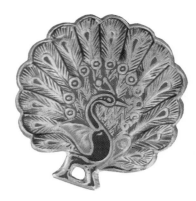

Clasps, unmarked, c. 1930. Top: Dragonfly, orange wings with black body, basse-taille enamel, 2" x .75". $25-30. Bottom: Circle of white enamel, miniature fans with green, red, and pink enamel flowers in center circle, 2.75" x 1.25". $20-25.

Clasp, unmarked, c. 1925. Two half circles, champlevé enameled black, blue, and white diamonds and squares, separated by two bezel set black, pressed glass stones, 2.25" x 1.75". $35-40.

Buckle, marked " IUOIP," c. 1945. Peacock, enameled cast brass, violet, red, and green colors, 2" x 2.25". $30-35.

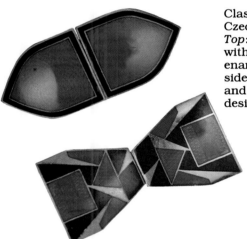

Clasps, marked, "Made in Czechoslovakia," c. 1935. *Top*: Five sided cloisonné, red with black trim, basse-taille enamel, 2.5" x 1". *Bottom*: Six sided cloisonn é, red, white, and blue in a geometric design, 2.5" x 1". $25-40 ea..

Clasp, unmarked, c. 1900. Red, blue, white, and green enamel on gold washed, stamped and pierced groundplate, bezel set green glass jewel at center, 3.5" x 2.25". $50-75. *Evelyn Gibbons collection.*

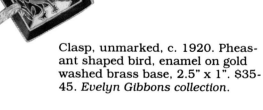

Clasp, unmarked, c. 1920. Pheasant shaped bird, enamel on gold washed brass base, 2.5" x 1". $35-45. *Evelyn Gibbons collection.*

Clasp, marked "34," c. 1920. Heart shaped, enamel and millifiori on a brass base, 2" x 1". $40-50. *Mrs. W.C. Hewitt collection.*

Clasp, unmarked, c. 1930. Enamel on gold washed brass base, flowers, 2" x 1". $20-25. *Louise Cook collection.*

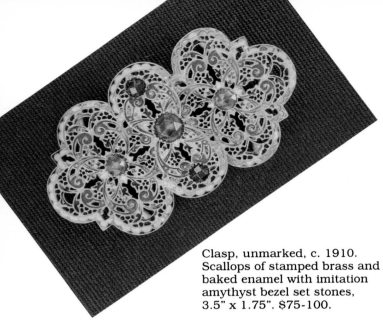

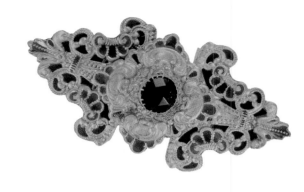

Clasp, unmarked, c. 1910. Scallops of stamped brass and baked enamel with imitation amythyst bezel set stones, 3.5" x 1.75". $75-100.

Clasp, unmarked, c. 1900. Stamped brass pattern with enamel trim, emerald green faceted pressed glass, bezel set, 3.5" x 1.75". $50-75.

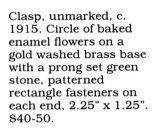

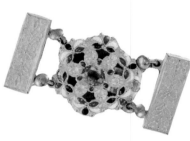

Clasp, unmarked, c. 1930. Ovals of enameled stamped brass with pavé set green, red, and amber glass stones with one red cabochon, bezel set and centered, 2" x 1.25". $15-25.

Clasp, unmarked, c. 1915. Circle of baked enamel flowers on a gold washed brass base with a prong set green stone, patterned rectangle fasteners on each end, 2.25" x 1.25". $40-50.

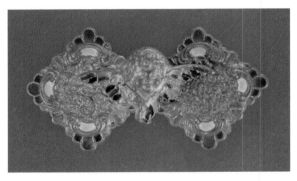

Clasp, unmarked, c. 1890. Triple circles of faceted cut steels riveted to a brass base, surrounding champlevé enameled flowers, 2.75" x 1.25". $50-75.

Clasp, unmarked, c. 1890. WINGED CHERUBIM, gold washed brass base with enamel trim, 3" x 5.5". $35-50.

Clasp, unmarked, c. 1925. Black and white enameled overlapping flowers, 3.25" x 1.75". $25-30.

Clasp, unmarked, c. 1925. Circle shaped cross hatch design, multi-colored enamel, 1.75" x 1.25". $15-30.

Clasp, unmarked, c. 1900. Pink enameled posies on gold washed stamped brass, 3" x 1.5". $20-30.

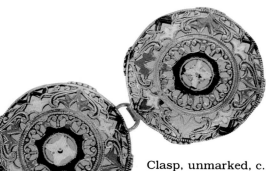

Clasp, unmarked, c. 1910. Stamped brass circles, flower pattern with painted multi-color enamel, 3.5" x 1.75". $35-40.

Clasp, unmarkled, c. 1935. Rectangle shaped, oxidized metal front with etched pattern, silver filled and black enamel, riveted to a metal backplate, 2.75" x 2". $30-35.

Clasp, unmarked, c. 1955. Triangle shaped with black domed center with black and white rays of painted enamel, 5" x 3". $20-30.

Clasp, unmarked, c. 1910. Stamped brass rolled edge, patterned and multi-colored enamel, 4.5" x 2.5". $35-45.

Clasp, unmarked, c. 1910. Oval shaped with scalloped edges and a green pressed glass center stone, white enamel trim, 3" x 2". $35-40.

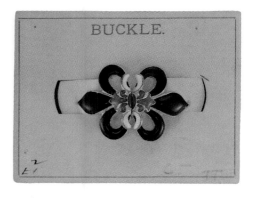

Clasp, unmarked, on card marked, "Buckle," c. 1920. Fleur-de-lis motif, blue, white, and green enamel on a gold brass base, 1.5" x 1", card is 1.75" x 2.25" $35-50.

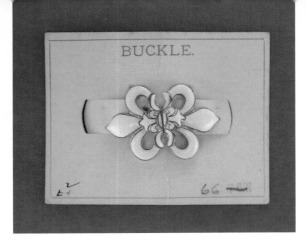

Clasp, unmarked, on card marked, "Buckle," c. 1920. Fleur-de-lis motif, white enamel on a gold brass base, 1.5" x 1", card is 1.75" x 2.25". $35-50.

Clasp, unmarked, c. 1920. Victorian style, gold washed brass with pink, blue, and green enamel trim, and prong set red cabochon, centered, 3" x 1.5". $35-50.

Clasp, unmarked, c. 1920. Egyptian pictorial, blue, white, and red enamel on brass, pierced groundplate, 3.75" x 1.75". $75-100. *Evelyn Gibbons collection.*

Belt, unmarked, c. 1900. Gold washed brass clasp, red, white, green, and black enamel on a flower patterned circle, fastened to a bronze satin cloth, clasp is 1.75" sq., over all length 29". $50-75.

Chapter Three
Buckles Made From Plastic

Plastic is a synthetically produced compound that when heated can be molded and shaped. Besides being molded, plastic can be sliced, ground and carved into various shapes. It is lightweight, durable and easy to manufacture in mass quantities. Plastic can be used alone or as a base for metal, glass and any other type of decorative material. There are two types of plastic materials: Thermoplastic substances which can be reheated and remolded, and thermosetting substances which are permanently hard and unmoldable once subjected to heat.

The oldest form of plastic, a semisynthetic thermoplastic called *celluloid*, was invented in 1869 by John Wesley Hyatt as an imitation of ivory and is a mixture of nitrocellulose and camphor. It was first used for billiard balls, but was found to be too brittle. It was soon used as an imitation for glass, jade, coral, marble and several other natural materials in jewelry making. Available in hundreds of colors, celluloid was popular in the 1870s through the 1930s for jewelry.

Bakelite, a thermosetting substance, was the first entirely man-made plastic. It was invented in 1907 by Belgian chemist Dr. Leo Hendrik Baekeland. It, too, was used as an imitation for more expensive materials in jewelry making. In the 1930s, Bakelite jewelry could be found in most prestigious stores around the world and by 1936, it was estimated two-thirds of all costume jewelry was made from Bakelite.

After World War II, Bakelite was no longer cost-effective to produce and another form of plastic, Lucite, gained in popularity. Lucite is a trade name for an acrylic resin introduced by DuPont in 1937. It is a clear plastic that can be tinted with a wide range of transparent to opaque colors. Today's terminology for clear plastic is Plexiglas and it is still in wide use today.

It can sometimes be difficult to tell the difference between the various types of plastic, but with close inspection using smell and sight they can be readily distinguished. When either rubbed or pricked with a hot needle in an inconspicuous spot, celluloid will release a camphor odor, Bakelite has a distinct acrid odor and Lucite is odorless. Using sight and feel, celluloid is thin-layered, light and delicate looking, while Bakelite is dense, solid and heavy, and Lucite is translucent.

Clasp, unmarked, c.1930. Mme. Chrysanthemum, stamped brass set in a Bakelite base, 4.25" x 2.25". $30-40.

Clasp, unmarked, 1850-1900. Oriental Matron, stamped brass figure riveted to Bakelite base with faceted cut steels in a circle of brass studs, 4.5" x 2.25". $50-75.

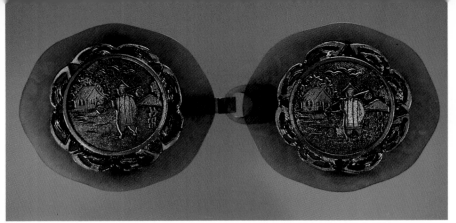

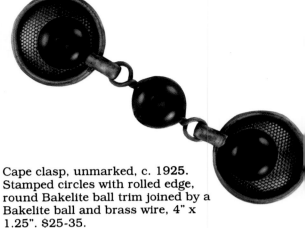

Clasp, unmarked, c. 1910. Chinese peasant, carrying baskets on a pole, village scene in background , stamped brass in low relief mounted to a Bakelite base, 6" x 2.5". $65-85.

Cape clasp, unmarked, c. 1925. Stamped circles with rolled edge, round Bakelite ball trim joined by a Bakelite ball and brass wire, 4" x 1.25". $25-35.

Cape clasp, unmarked, c. 1925. Stamped brass, simple pattern with five sided Bakelite piece mounted to base with small filigree trim, joined by two brass rope rings and link, 5.25" x 1.5". $30-35.

Cape clasp, unmarked, c. 1920. Oxidized stamped brass, starburst pattern and tiny plastic beads, on a domed Bakelite disc, joined by four oval brass rings, 5.75" x 1.75". $35-45.

Cape clasp, unmarked, c. 1920. Round stamped brass filigree pattern on cupped Bakelite disc, joined by two brass rings and a link, 5.25" x 1.75". $35-40.

Cape clasp, unmarked, c. 1910. Silver luster, pressed patterned glass set in a cupped Bakelite mount, mounted to a steel plate and joined by a double row of chains, 6.25" x 1.5". $40-50.

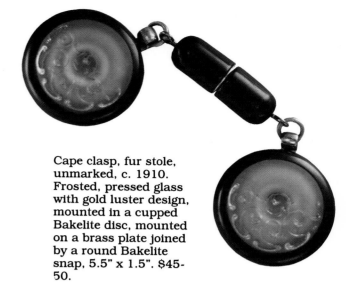

Cape clasp, unmarked, c. 1900. Iris, stamped brass mounted on a Bakelite disc, joined by three brass rings and two links, 6" x 1.75". $35-45.

Cape clasp, fur stole, unmarked, c. 1910. Frosted, pressed glass with gold luster design, mounted in a cupped Bakelite disc, mounted on a brass plate joined by a round Bakelite snap, 5.5" x 1.5". $45-50.

Cape clasp, unmarked, c. 1920. Round, stamped brass with a waffle pattern mounted on a Bakelite disc, joined by a single ring, 4.75" x 1.75". $30-35.

Cape clasp, unmarked, c. 1910. Gold luster, patterned pressed glass mounted in a cupped Bakelite disc, joined by double looped brass roping, 6" x 1.5". $45-50.

Cape clasp, unmarked, c. 1925. Tulip shaped, Bakelite, joined by a single brass ring, 5" x 1.25". $30-35.

Cape clasp, unmarked, c. 1920. Black Bakelite roses, joined by double rows of double linked brass ovals, rope shape, 7" x 1.75". $35-45.

Cape, clasp, unmarked, c. 1930. Oxidized, stamped brass shell design, mounted in a red Bakelite cupped disc, joined by three brass, rope shaped, ovals and two links, 5.75" x 1.5". $35-40.

Cape clasp, unmarked, c. 1910. Quarter moon shaped, oxidized stamped brass, flower pattern on leaf shaped brown Bakelite, joined by a single rope shaped ring, 4.5" x 1.75". $35-40.

Cape clasp, unmarked, c. 1900. Round, black luster pressed glass, with a sunburst pattern, bezel set in a black Bakelite base joined by five hammered metal loops, 5.25" x 1.5". $60-

Cape clasp, unmarked, c. 1930. Stamped brass, vine design on black Bakelite, joined by four brass ovals, 4.75" x 1.25". $25-30.

Cape clasp, unmarked, c. 1935. Pewter sunburst with red plastic center on a black Bakelite triangle, joined by a single ring, 5" x 1.75". $20-25.

Cape clasp, unmarked, c. 1930. Carved black Bakelite with recessed metal trims, joined by four double metal loops, 6" x 1.75". $25-30.

Cape clasp, unmarked, c. 1925. Acorn shaped black Bakelite, joined by two Bakelite rings, 5.25" x 1". $20-25.

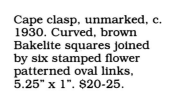

Cape clasp, unmarked, c. 1930. Plated stamped brass disc, on a green Bakelite disc, joined by two plate rings and a link, 5" x 1.5". $25-30.

Cape clasp, unmarked, c. 1930. Curved, brown Bakelite squares joined by six stamped flower patterned oval links, 5.25" x 1". $20-25.

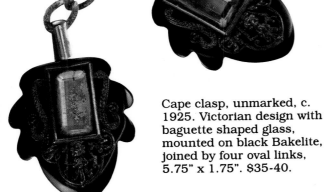

Cape clasp, unmarked, c. 1925. Victorian design with baguette shaped glass, mounted on black Bakelite, joined by four oval links, 5.75" x 1.75". $35-40.

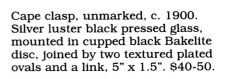

Cape clasp, unmarked, c. 1900. Silver luster black pressed glass, mounted in cupped black Bakelite disc, joined by two textured plated ovals and a link, 5" x 1.5". $40-50.

Cape clasp, unmarked, c. 1900. Frosted and etched, pyramid designed pressed glass recessed in a carved black Bakelite base, joined by five plated metal links, 5.5" x 1". $40-45.

Cape clasp, unmarked, c. 1900. Silver luster black pressed glass, set in a cupped brown Bakelite base, mounted to a brass plate, joined by a double loop of brass rope, 6" x 1.5". $45-50.

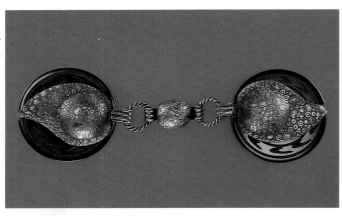

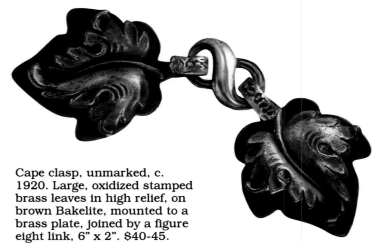

Cape clasp, unmarked, c. 1910. Oxidized stamped brass leaves with flower pattern, mounted on a carved, black Bakelite base, joined by two wire rope loops and a cupped link, 6.5" x 2". $40-45.

Cape clasp, unmarked, c. 1920. Large, oxidized stamped brass leaves in high relief, on brown Bakelite, mounted to a brass plate, joined by a figure eight link, 6" x 2". $40-45.

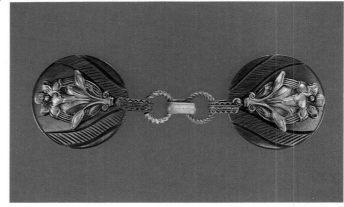

Cape clasp, unmarked, c. 1920. Large, oxidized stamped brass flowers with overlapping petals on a black Bakelite base, joined by a 1.25" formed loop, oxidized brass chain, 6" x 1.75". $45-50.

Cape clasp, unmarked, c. 1920. Stamped brass lilies in a vase in high relief, mounted on a carved brown Bakelite base, joined by two brass rope rings and a link, 5" x 1.75". $40-50.

Cape clasp, unmarked, c. 1935. Eight petals, black Bakelite flowers, joined by a single loop, 4" x 1.5". $10-15.

Cape clasp, unmarked, c. 1935. Black Bakelite triangle, joined by a black Bakelite knot, 6.25" x 1.25". $10-20.

Cape clasp, unmarked, c. 1930. Pewter, flower leaf design, with three prong set blue stones on a black Bakelite base, joined by five hammered brass rings, 5.5" x 1.5". $35-40.

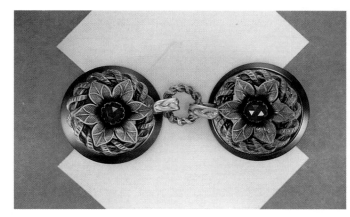

Cape clasp, unmarked, c. 1920. Six petal flowers with blue prong set stones at center in a circle of vines, oxidized stamped brass, joined by a vine shaped brass ring, 4.25" x 1.75". $50-60.

Cape clasp, unmarked, c. 1920. Oxidized stamped brass, circle of leaves and flowers intertwined, centered with a domed sun star, mounted on a purple Bakelite base, 6.5" x 3". $45-50.

Cape clasp, unmarked, c. 1930. Oxidized stamped brass, shield design, on brown Bakelite, with a carved scalloped edge, joined by two brass rings and a link, 5.25" x 1.75". $35-45.

Cape clasp, unmarked, c. 1920. Victorian style, stamped brass dome set in brown Bakelite patterned base, joined by a brass rope ring, 4.5" x 1.75". $30-40.

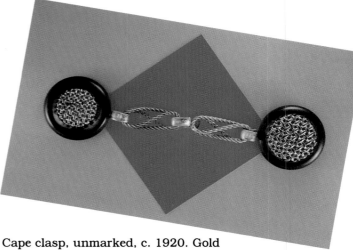

Cape clasp, unmarked, c. 1920. Three sided design, Victorian, oxidized stamped brass on a brown Bakelite base, joined by two plated rings and a link, 5" x 1.75". $35-40.

Cape clasp, unmarked, c. 1920. Gold luster pressed glass, woven design set in a cupped brown Bakelite base, joined by two double loop brass rope and a link, 6" x 1.5". $45-50.

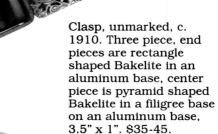

Clasp, unmarked, c. 1910. Three piece, end pieces are rectangle shaped Bakelite in an aluminum base, center piece is pyramid shaped Bakelite in a filigree base on an aluminum base, 3.5" x 1". $35-45.

Cape clasp, unmarked, c. 1930. Oxidized stamped brass, sunflower on a triangle shaped carved Bakelite base, joined by a filigree link, 5.5" x 1.75". $35-40.

Clasp, unmarked, c. 1920. Carved dark brown Bakelite, flower with swirls, and carved triangles, with gold metal trim and beading, 3.75" x 1.75". $65-75.

Clasp, unmarked, c. 1920. Rounded, black Bakelite triangle with oxidized stamped brass leaves riveted to the top, 3" x 1.25". $30-45.

Clasp, unmarked, c. 1950. Flowers, black Bakelite with overlapping petals, 4" x 2". $35-40.

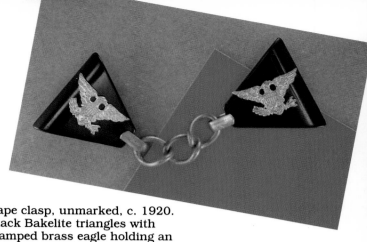

Cape clasp, unmarked, c. 1920. Black Bakelite triangles with stamped brass eagle holding an olive branch, joined by three brass oval links, 5" x 1.75". $40-50.

Clasp, unmarked, c. 1920. Black carved Bakelite rectangles, fan design at opposing corners, mounted on a brass plate, 3.25" x 2.25". $65-75.

Clasp, unmarked, c. 1930. Carved ducks on orange colored Bakelite circles, 3" x 1.75". $50-75.

Clasp, unmarked, c. 1930. Half round black Bakelite, with carved flower design on top, surrounded by a carved design, 2.25" x 1.25". $25-35.

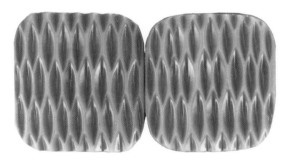

Clasp, unmarked, c. 1935. Coral colored rectangles, with pattern design, Bakelite, 3" x 1.75". $45-50.

Clasp, unmarked, c. 1930. Green Bakelite ovals mounted to a plated metal back, joined by two hooks with balled ends, 3" x 1". $25-35.

Clasp, unmarked, c. 1930. Carved yellow Bakelite circles, leaf pattern with .75" hole at each end and two leaf cutouts, 3.5" x 1.5". $50-60.

Clasp, unmarked, c. 1925. Large black Bakelite discs, covered with a pewter filigree flower design, 6" x 3.25". $35-45.

Clasp, unmarked, c. 1945. Carved yellow Bakelite with a "D" shape cutout in the middle of each half, 2.75" x 1.75". $45-50.

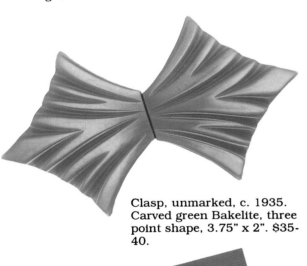

Clasp, unmarked, c. 1935. Carved green Bakelite, three point shape, 3.75" x 2". $35-40.

Clasp, unmarked, c. 1930. Brown covered white Bakelite with white leaves on a stem, six rhinestones set in each leaf, 2.5" x 1.5". $45-50.

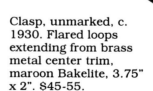

Clasp, unmarked, c. 1930. Red Bakelite bars with silver metal trim pieces, 2.5" x 1.5". $35-40.

Clasp, unmarked, c. 1910. Black Bakelite circles with fan design, 4.25" x 2.75". $30-35.

Clasp, unmarked, c. 1930. Flared loops extending from brass metal center trim, maroon Bakelite, 3.75" x 2". $45-55.

Clasp, unmarked, c. 1940. Green Bakelite, ribbon look design, 3" x 1.25". $25-35.

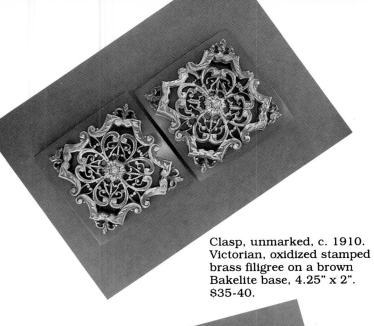

Clasp, unmarked, c. 1910. Victorian, oxidized stamped brass filigree on a brown Bakelite base, 4.25" x 2". $35-40.

Clasp, unmarked, c. 1920. Oxidized stamped brass, square shape, flower design, on black Bakelite base, 3.5" x 1.75". $30-35.

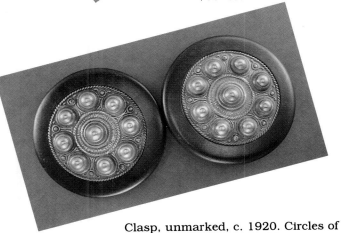

Clasp, unmarked, c. 1920. Circles of rounded points, stamped brass on a cupped composite base, 4.75" x 2.5". $45-55.

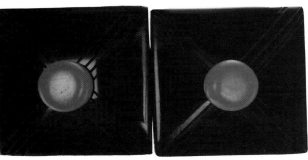

Clasp, unmarked, c. 1930. Bakelite squares with carved "x" and red buttons centered, 3.75" x 2". $25-30.

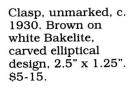

Clasp, unmarked, c. 1930. Brown on white Bakelite, carved elliptical design, 2.5" x 1.25". $5-15.

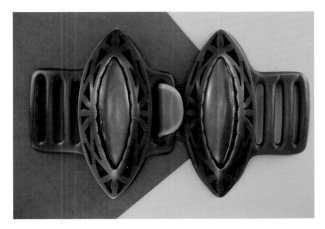

Clasp, unmarked, c. 1930. Layered Bakelite, cat eye design in a pattern base, with a curved hook, and triple slot for cloth, 5.25" x 3.25". $50-75.

Buckle, unmarked, c. 1935. Black over white Bakelite with four pointed carved stars, single closure, 2.5" dia..$20-25.

Clasp, unmarked, c. 1930. Brown Bakelite, layered, Art Deco on top layer and formed hook on bottom layer, unusual piece, 3.75" x 2.5". $50-55.

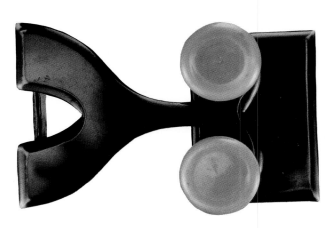

Clasp, unmarked, c. 1935. Black Bakelite, double hook, fastens around two gray buttons, 3.75" x 2.25". $35-45.

Clasp, marked, "Pat.pend.," c. 1945. Red Bakelite rectangles, 2.5" x 1.75". $35-40.

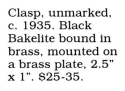

Clasp, unmarked, c. 1945. Black Bakelite ripple design, 2.75" x 1.25". $30-35.

Clasp, unmarked, c. 1940. Cut to shape, orange Bakelite with pearl inlay, 2.25" x 2". $35-40.

Clasp, unmarked, c. 1935. Black Bakelite bound in brass, mounted on a brass plate, 2.5" x 1". $25-35.

Buckle, unmarked, c. 1940. Brown Bakelite, open center, single closure, 3" x 2.5". $25-30.

Clasp, unmarked, c. 1935. Black Bakelite shell design, joined to a green Bakelite bar with a plated metal strap, 6" x 2". $45-55.

Clasp, unmarked, c. 1935. Brown Bakelite carved leaf design, 3.5" x 1.25". $35-40.

Clasp, unmarked, c. 1935. Green Bakelite overlapping leave shape, with green Bakelite button set in pearl, 4" x 2". $55-70.

Clasp, unmarked, c. 1935. Green Bakelite flower design, 2.75" x 1.5". $40-50.

Clasp, unmarked, c. 1920. Dark green Bakelite triangle design, with stamped brass design, 2.25" x .75". $15-20.

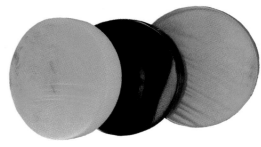

Clasp, unmarked, c. 1945. Brown Bakelite carved leaf design, 4.75" x 1.75". $35-40.

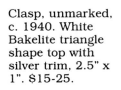

Clasp, unmarked, c. 1930. Black Bakelite, with carved design on top and sides, 3" x 1.5". $25-35.

Clasp, unmarked, c. 1935. Amber, black, and orange, Bakelite circles, 3" x 1.5". $45-55.

Clasp, unmarked, c. 1940. White Bakelite triangle shape top with silver trim, 2.5" x 1". $15-25.

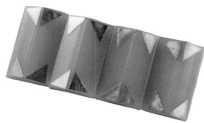

Clasp, unmarked, c. 1940. Red Bakelite half round shape, 2" x 2". $30-35.

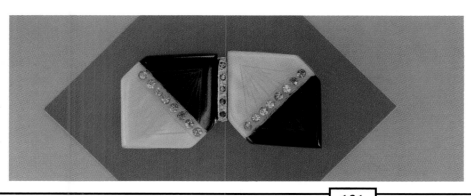

Clasp, unmarked, c. 1935. Brown and white Bakelite triangles with a carved pattern, rows of pavé set rhinestones at each center, 2.5" x 1.25". $35-40.

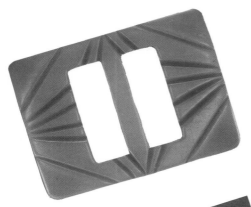

Buckle, un-marked, c. 1930. Amber colored Bakelite, carved pattern, 2.5" x 1.75". $5-10.

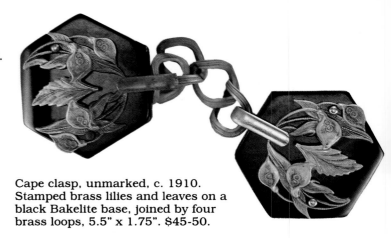

Cape clasp, unmarked, c. 1910. Stamped brass lilies and leaves on a black Bakelite base, joined by four brass loops, 5.5" x 1.75". $45-50.

Cape clasp, unmarked, c. 1920. Oxidized stamped brass, flower and petals with a brown glass center, joined by four brass oval links, 6" x 1.75". $45-55.

Cape clasp, unmarked, c. 1900. Oxidized stamped brass, five petal flower with brown glass center on a filigree circle, mounted on a brown Bakelite base, joined by a brass stamped patterned figure eight, with flower bud at center, 6" x 2". $55-65.

Clasp, dress clip set, unmarked, c. 1935. Hard-wood center with orange Bakelite side pieces, brass trim across the center, clasp is 3.75" x 1.75", clip is 1.5" x 2". $50-75.

Cape clasp, button, unmarked, c. 1920. Gibson girl in brass on a Bakelite base, joined by three brass loops, 5.75" x 1.75", button, 1.75" dia.. $50-75.

Cape clasp, button, unmarked, c. 1920. Oxidized stamped rolled brass discs on a Bakelite base, joined by two rope rings and a link, 5.75" x 1.75", button, 1.75" dia.. $50-60.

Cape clasp, button, unmarked, c. 1920. Oxidized stamped brass, flowers with brass ball center on a Bakelite base, joined by a flower bud link, 4.75" x 1.5", button, 1.75" dia.. $50-60.

Cape clasp, button set, unmarked, c. 1920. Stamped brass, lilies and foliage on brown Bakelite with an imitation coral glass stone, joined by a single ring, 5" x 1.75", button, 1.75" dia.. $50-75.

Cape clasp, button, un-marked, c. 1920. Brass roses on a carved brown Bakelite base, joined by three pat-terned brass loops, 5.5" x 1.75", button 1.75" dia.. $50-60.

Cape clasp, button, unmarked, c. 1925. Pewter foliage on a brown Bakelite base with prong set blue stones, joined by five hammered brass rings, 6" x 1.75", button, 1.75" dia.. $40-50.

Clasp, unmarked, c. 1930. Eight sided designed pattern, white on red Bakelite, 2.75" x 1.5". $25-20.

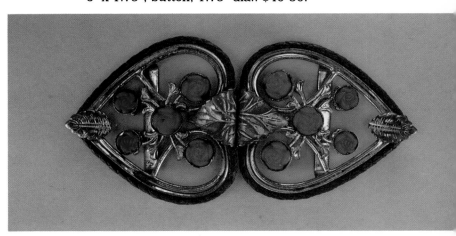

Clasp, unmarked, c. 1955. Heart shaped, gold washed brass base, trimmed in red leather with brass leaves and red bezel set Bakelite roses, 4.25" x 2". $45-55.

Buckle, unmarked, c. 1935. White sunflowers and foliage on an orange Bakelite base, 3.5" x 2". $15-25.

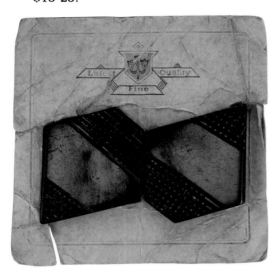

Clasp, unmarked, on card marked,"LaMode buckle, $5.00, 4121 Green," c. 1950. Square shaped green Bakelite with flower pattern, 2" x 4", card is 4" x 4.25". $30-45.

Buckle, button set, unmarked, on card marked, "Quality Merite Buttons, reg.U.S. pat off," c. 1930. Red Bakelite, buckle with single crossbar and four buttons, buckle is 2" x 1.75", buttons .8"dia., card is 2.75" x 7". $15-25.

Clasp, unmarked, on card marked, "Latest Quality Fine," c. 1920. Black Bakelite, five sided, 2.5" x 1.5", card is 3"sq.. $15-25.

Clasp, unmarked, on card marked, "Costume Ornament for Dress. Coat. Hat, NRA we do our best, Well Made Safety," c. 1950. Oblong shaped, green Bakelite with silver trim, recessed at cross corners, 2.75" x 1.25", card is 4" x 3.25". $15-25.

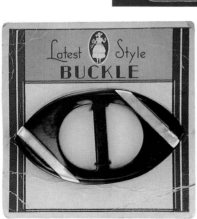

Buckle, unmarked, on card marked "Latest Style BUCKLE," c. 1935. Oblong shaped, black Bakelite with pearl inlay, 3.25" x 2.25", card is 3.75" sq.. $15-25.

Clasp, unmarked, c. 1930. Pair of green Bakelite birds, 4.5" x 2". $35-50. *Mrs. W.C. Hewitt collection.*

Cape clasp, unmarked, c. 1920. Carved Bakelite owls joined by a single brass ring, 4.5" x 1.75" $45-60. *Evelyn Gibbons collection.*

Clasp, unmarked, c. 1940. Orange and white Bakelite discs with Bakelite pins going thru double eyeloops, 2.25" x 1.5". $35-45.

Cape clasp, unmarked, c. 1935. Carved black Bakelite, leaf pattern joined by two round links, 6" x 1.75". $35-50.

Cape clasp, unmarked, c. 1930. Stamped brass circles with a center peak on carved Bakelite, joined by a double brass loop, 5" x 1.75". $35-50.

Cape clasp, unmarked, c. 1930. Tulip shaped flower, brown Bakelite joined by brass rectangle links, 5.75" x 1.75". $35-50.

Cape clasp, unmarked, c. 1930. Brown Bakelite flowers joined by brass rope ovals, 7" x 1.5". $35-50.

Set, clasp and buttons, unmarked, c. 1930. Bakelite, beige circle on an orange circle, 3.75" x 2". Matching buttons, 1.5"dia.. $35-50.

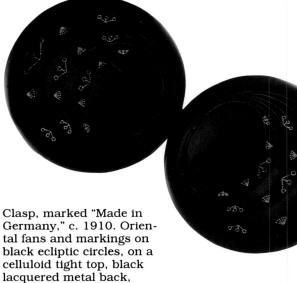

Clasp, marked "Germany,"c. 1910. Chinese characters surrounded by fish and flower design printed on a celluloid tight top, black lacquered metal back, 5.5" x 2.75". $35-45.

Clasp, marked "Made in Germany," c. 1910. Oriental fans and markings on black ecliptic circles, on a celluloid tight top, black lacquered metal back, 5.25" x 2.75". $35-45.

Clasp, unmarked, c. 1930. Oriental man and woman, cast oxidized brass figures on a gold,orange, and brown blended background, on a convex celluloid base, 5.5" x 2.75". $45-65.

Clasp, unmarked, c. 1935. Oriental woman with fan, flowers, trees, and characters, on a celluloid tight top, black lacquered metal back, 5.25" x 2.75". $35-50.

Clasp, unmarked, c. 1890-1910. Lake and mountain scene, imitation of Japanese lacquer work, hand painted with thick gilt, 5" x 2.5". $40-60.

Clasp, unmarked, c. 1890-1910. Mme. Chrysanthemum, hand painted silver on celluloid, 5.75" x 2.25". $30-40.

Buckle, unmarked, c. 1900. Oriental woman serving tea, celluloid on plastic base, 3" x 3". $40-50.

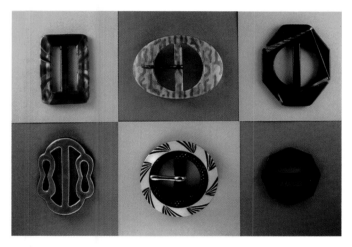

Misc. celluloid buckles, various shapes and colors, $5-10 ea..

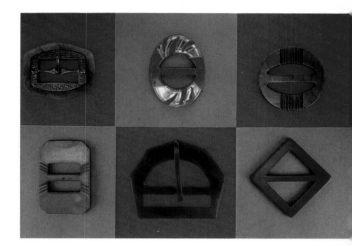

Misc. celluloid buckles, various shapes and colors, $5-10 ea..

Clasp, unmarked, c. 1925. Tight top celluloid, tan and black oriental scene, 3.5" x 1.75". $50-65.

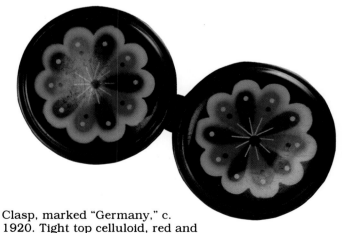

Clasp, marked "Germany," c. 1920. Tight top celluloid, red and green petals on a yellow background, 4" x 2". $25-35.

Clasp, unmarked, c. 1935. White celluloid circles with red and black squares, 3..5" x 1.75". $15-20.

Clasp, marked "Made in Germany," c. 1925. Tight top celluloid, brown edging, offset squares with blended green, gold, and tan colors, black lacquered back plate, 4.5" x 2.25". $30-35.

Clasp, marked "Germany," c. 1920. Tight top celluloid, brown with green hot air balloon design, black lacquered metal back, 3.75" x 1.75" $25-30.

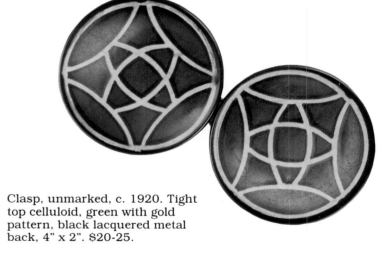

Clasp, unmarked, c. 1920. Tight top celluloid, green with gold pattern, black lacquered metal back, 4" x 2". $20-25.

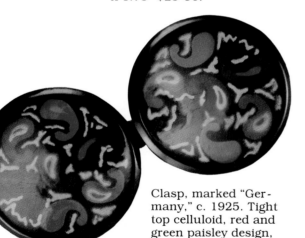

Clasp, marked "Germany," c. 1925. Tight top celluloid, red and green paisley design, black lacquered metal back, 4" x 2". $20-25.

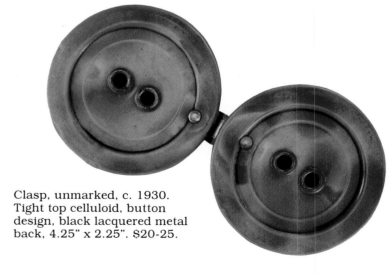

Clasp, unmarked, c. 1930. Tight top celluloid, button design, black lacquered metal back, 4.25" x 2.25". $20-25.

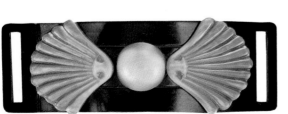

Clasp, unmarked, c. 1935. Interconnecting black celluloid base with imitation shell design, separated by a half round piece of celluloid, 3.5" x 1". $30-35.

Clasp, unmarked, c. 1935. Celluloid rectangles, triangle designs in orange, yellow, and ivory colors, 3" x 1.25". $15-25.

Clasp, unmarked, c. 1935. Celluloid circles with a pattern design, diamond design at center, 5.25" x 3". $30-40.

Clasp, marked "Made in Czechoslovakia," c. 1920. Tight top celluloid, blue and white paisley in a stamped brass base, 3.5" x 1". $25-30.

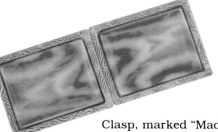

Clasp, marked "Made in Czechoslovakia," c. 1920. Tight top celluloid, red and pink colors in a stamped brass base, 2.5" x 1". $25-30.

Clasp, marked "Czechoslovakia," c. 1930. Art Deco, black, gold, and gray colors on celluloid on a silver on brass base, 2.25" x 1". $25-30.

Clasp, marked "Made in Czechoslovakia," c. 1920. Green celluloid in a brass filigree base, 2.5" x 1". $25-30.

Clasp, marked "Made in Czechoslovakia," c. 1930. Art Deco, tan and brown celluloid on triangle shaped brass base, 2.75" x 1". $25-30.

Clasp, marked "Made in Czechoslovakia," c. 1930. Art Deco, green and lime colors in a brass base, rectangle shape, 3" x 1.25". $25-30.

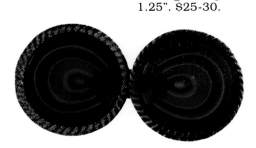

Clasp, marked "Made in Czechoslovakia, GES.GESCHUTZT," c. 1930. Art Deco, red and pink circles with a green and black diamond at center in a circular brass base, 3" x 1.5". $25-30.

Clasp, marked "Made in Czechoslovakia, GES.GESCHUTZT," c. 1930. Green celluloid in a six sided brass base with a filigree flower design on top, 2.25" x 1.25". $25-30.

Clasp, marked "Made in Czechoslovakia," c. 1930. Art Deco, black and gray celluloid in a plated brass base, 2.75" x 1". $25-30.

Clasp, marked "GES.GESCHUTZT," c. 1925. Green celluloid with gold stripes in pointed brass base with brass filigree at the center, 2.75" x 1". $25-30.

Clasp, marked "Czechoslov," c. 1930. Brown celluloid with plated triangle in a six sided plated metal base, 2.25" x 1.25". $25-30.

Clasp, marked "Czechoslov," c. 1930. Tan celluloid with gold splash in a triangle shaped brass base with brass pattern at center, 2.5" x 1.5". $25-30.

Clasp, marked "Made in Czechoslovakia, GES. GESCHUTZT," c. 1930. Gray celluloid in a brass base with filigree pattern, 2.75" x 1". $25-30.

Clasp, unmarked, c. 1930. Black and silver celluloid in a rectangle shaped brass plated base, 3" x 1". $20-25.

Clasp, unmarked, c. 1930. Tan and black luster celluloid, pointed shape in a plated metal base, 3.5" x 1". $20-25.

Clasp, marked "Made in Germany," c. 1925. Red luster celluloid, pointed shape in a brass base, 3.25" x 1.25". $25-30.

Clasp, marked "Made in Germany," c. 1935. Green celluloid in a brass filigree sunburst of brass, rectangle shape, 2.5" x 1.25". $25-30.

Clasp, marked "Made in Germany," c. 1930. Brown celluloid in a teardrop shaped brass base, 3.25" x 1.25". $25-30.

Clasp, marked "Made in Germany," c. 1930. Art Deco, brown and tan patterned celluloid in a brass base, 2.25" x 1". $25-30.

Clasp, marked "Made in Germany," c. 1925. Brown celluloid with white square and gold pattern in a brass base, rectangle shape, 2.5" x 1". $25-30.

Clasp, marked "Germany," c. 1930. Acorn shape, Art Deco, brown and tan celluloid, 2.5" x 1". $25-30.

Clasp, unmarked, c. 1930. Art Deco, oblong green and lime colored angles, 2.25" x 1". $20-25.

Clasp, marked "Czechoslov," c. 1930. Rust and beige celluloid on a metal base, 3" x 1.25". $25-30.

Clasp, marked "Germany," c. 1930. Art Deco, red and black celluloid, angle pattern, 3" x 1". $25-30.

Clasp, unmarked, c. 1920. Tinted stamped celluloid, scarab body, on an oxidized stamped brass base in the shape of wings and legs, 2.75" x 2.5". $50-75.

Clasp, marked "Made in Germany," c. 1930. Celluloid on a brass base, black stripes across brown, tan and red rays, 2.75" x 1.25". $20-25.

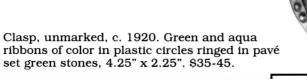

Clasp, unmarked, c. 1920. Green and aqua ribbons of color in plastic circles ringed in pavé set green stones, 4.25" x 2.25". $35-45.

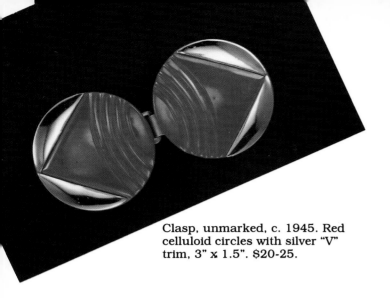

Clasp, unmarked, c. 1945. Red celluloid circles with silver "V" trim, 3" x 1.5". $20-25.

Clasp and button set, unmarked, c. 1940. Red celluloid in a plated matal trim, 3" x 1.5", buttons are 1.5" dia. and .8" dia. $15-20.

Clasp, unmarked, c. 1940. Red and white celluloid, round discs on a metal back, 2.25" x 1.25". $15-25.

Clasp, unmarked, c. 1920. Enameled stamped brass circles of impatients on a celluloid base, 3.5" x 3". $40-50.

Clasp, unmarked, c. 1935. Oblong shaped, layered celluloid with etched flower design, 2.5" x 1.5". $15-20.

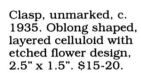

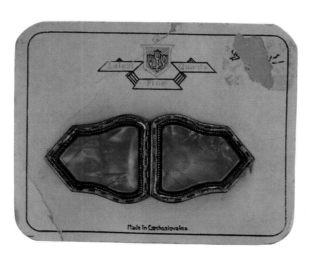

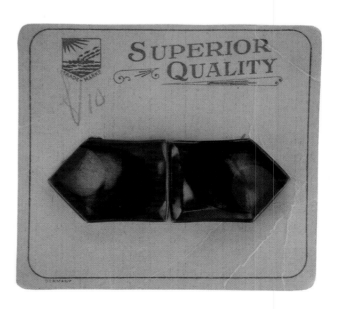

Clasp, marked "Czechoslovakia," on card marked, "Latest Fine Quality, Made in Czechoslovakia," c. 1935. Red celluloid in a brass base, 2.5" x 1", card is 3.25" x 2.75". $20-30.

Clasp, marked "Germany," on card marked, "Superior Quality," c. 1935. Green and black colors tight top celluloid, five sided, 3" x 1", card is 3.75" x 3.25". $20-35.

Clasp, button set, marked "Czechoslovakia," on card marked, "Fashionable Dress Set, Latest Style, Made in Czechoslovakia," c. 1935. Round shaped gold on brown patterned design, tight top celluloid, clasp 2.25" x 1.25", buttons .75" dia, card is 4.25" x 3". $25-40.

Clasp, unmarked, on card marked, "Novelty Ornament," c. 1935. Black and blue interconnecting triangles, celluloid, 2" x 1.75", card is 3.5" x 3.25". $5-15.

Buckle, marked "Germany," on card marked, "LaMode, B, " c. 1930. Oblong shaped, green colors, tight top celluloid on a metal base, 2.25" x 1.75". $15-25.

Clasp, unmarked, c. 1935. Brown oval plastic base with celluloid fruit trim, 4.5" x 2.5". $35-50. *Evelyn Gibbons collection.*

Clasp, unmarked, 1920. Gold washed stamped brass discs with high relief, celluloid, Egyptian heads, 5.25" x 2.5". $50-75. *Annie Frazier collection.*

Clasps, unmarked, c. 1925. Four bubble celluloid, base metal, 1.75" x 1". $10-15 ea..

Clasp, marked "Pat. 2108. 905," c. 1950. Red celluloid flowers in a tree shape, 5.25" x 1.75". $10-15. *Louise Cook collection.*

Clasp, marked "Germany," c. 1945. Round, blue circles of plastic with gray and beige squares fastened to the top, 2" x 1". $5-10. *Connie Fitzner collection.*

Buckle, unmarked, c. 1920. Oblong shaped yellow plastic with a single closure, 4.25" x 2.75". $10-20. *Connie Fitzner collection.*

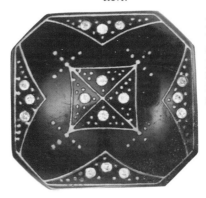

Buckle, belt ornament, unmarked, c. 1925. Square shaped, etched pattern on plastic with pavé set rhinestones, 2.25" sq.. $15-25. *Connie Fitzner collection.*

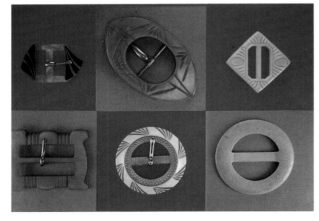

Buckles, unmarked, c. 1920-1940. Various shapes and colors of commmon plastic buckles, $5-10 ea..

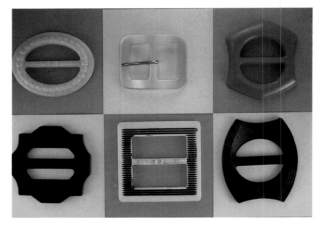

Buckles, unmarked, c. 1920-1940. Various shapes and colors of common plastic buckles, $5-10 ea.

Cape clasp, unmarked, c. 1925. Plated stamped brass leaf design, mounted to a yellow Lucite base joined by two plated rope rings and a link, 5.5" x 1.75". $30-35.

Cape clasp, unmarked, c. 1920. Stamped brass coiled rope pattern, imitation tortoise base joined by a single brass ring, 4.75" x 1.75". $35-40.

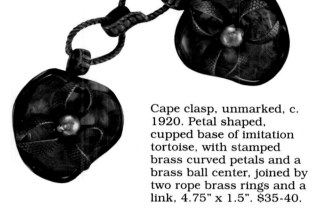

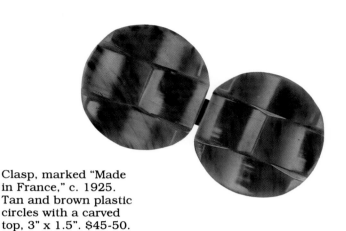

Cape clasp, unmarked, c. 1920. Petal shaped, cupped base of imitation tortoise, with stamped brass curved petals and a brass ball center, joined by two rope brass rings and a link, 4.75" x 1.5". $35-40.

Clasp, marked "Made in France," c. 1925. Tan and brown plastic circles with a carved top, 3" x 1.5". $45-50.

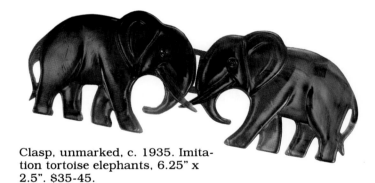

Clasp, marked "Germany," c. 1930. Plastic, muti-color brown with silver metal trim, cut to shape, 2.5"x 1.25". $15-25.

Clasp, unmarked, c. 1935. Imitation tortoise elephants, 6.25" x 2.5". $35-45.

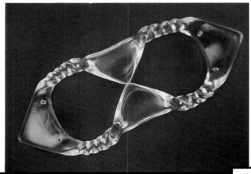

Clasp, unmarked, c. 1935. White plastic elephants, 6.25" x 2.5". $35-45.

Clasp, unmarked, c. 1920. Black plastic, scalloped fan design with vine design on a metal center plate, 3" x 2". $15-25.

Buckle, unmarked, c. 1940. Lucite, clear oblong formed and twisted center, 5.75" x 2.25". $20-30.

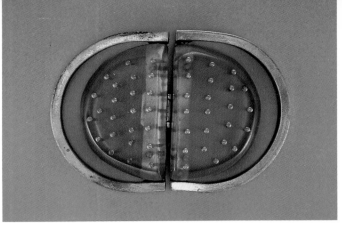

Clasp, unmarked, c. 1925. Yellow Lucite half circles pierced with rows of brads in a brass base, 3" x 2". $35-40.

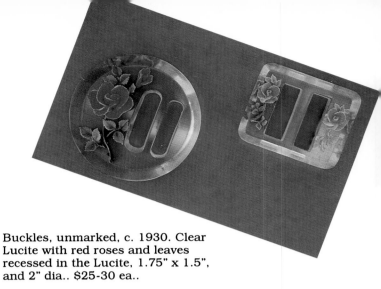

Buckles, unmarked, c. 1930. Clear Lucite with red roses and leaves recessed in the Lucite, 1.75" x 1.5", and 2" dia.. $25-30 ea..

Clasp, unmarked, c. 1930. Imitation amber, lucite rectangle bars, 1.25" x 2.5". $20-25.

Clasp, unmarked, c. 1940. Green and white marbled plastic cut to shape, with inlaid plastic strip, 2.75" x 1.5". $15-25.

Buckle, unmarked, c. 1910. Stamped and tinted celluloid, Art Nouveau, figure of woman with roses in her hair, prong set in a gold washed brass base, 1.75" sq.. $60-75.

Buckle, unmarked, c. 1930. Lucite with coral colored roses recessed in base, 1.75" sq. $25-30.

Clasp, pin set, marked "GREENBAUM," CA.1945. Gold washed plastic flowers with a circle of blue pavé set stones, 4.75" x 2", pin, 3.5" x 1.75". $30-40.

Clasp, button set, unmarked, c. 1950. Tan plastic circles with white flowers and leaves on a peaked center, 3.25" x 1.75", buttons, .8" dia. $15-20.

Clasp, button set,
unmarked, c. 1950.
Red on white plastic
circles with white
recessed flowers and
edge trim, 3.5" x
1.75", button, .8" dia.
$10-20.

Cape clasp ,button set, unmarked, c.
1945. Gray on black plastic circles, with
green bubble top at center, joined by
five plated brass loops, 6" x 1.75",
button, 2" dia.. $30-35.

Buckle, button set,
unmarked, c.
1950. Amber
colored circle with
serrated edge,
2.25" dia, button,
1.25" dia.. $5-10.

Clasp, button set, unmarked,
c. 1955. Plastic roses enamel
tipped, 3" x 1.5", button, .75"
dia.. $15-25.

Clasp, clip set, marked "Pat.pend,"
c. 1945. Pink plastic daisies with a
brown center, 4" x 2.25", clip,
2.25" dia.. $15-25.

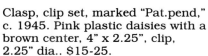

Clasp, unmarked, c.
1945. Red circles of
coiled rope plastic with
black coiled centers,
3.5" x 1.75". $10-20.

Clasp, unmarked, c. 1955.
Plastic, black flower pattern
on a red teardrop shaped
base, 4" x 1.5". $10-20.

Clasp, unmarked, c. 1935. Green plastic circles around dahlia shape center, 3.75" x 1.75". $15-25.

Clasp, unmarked, c. 1950. Orange plastic roses, 2.25" x 2.25". $10-20.

Clasp, unmarked, c. 1945. Gold washed cast base metal, roses with long leaves, 4.75" x 2". $35-45.

Clasp, unmarked, c. 1935. Gold on plastic, roses and flowers with green stone centers, with a foliage background, 4.5" x 2.25". $35-40.

Clasp, marked "GREENBAUM," c. 1945. Pink plastic roses on a purple plastic base, 4.75" x 1.75". $15-25.

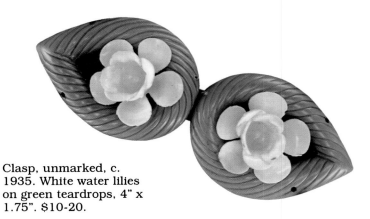

Clasp, unmarked, c. 1935. White water lilies on green teardrops, 4" x 1.75". $10-20.

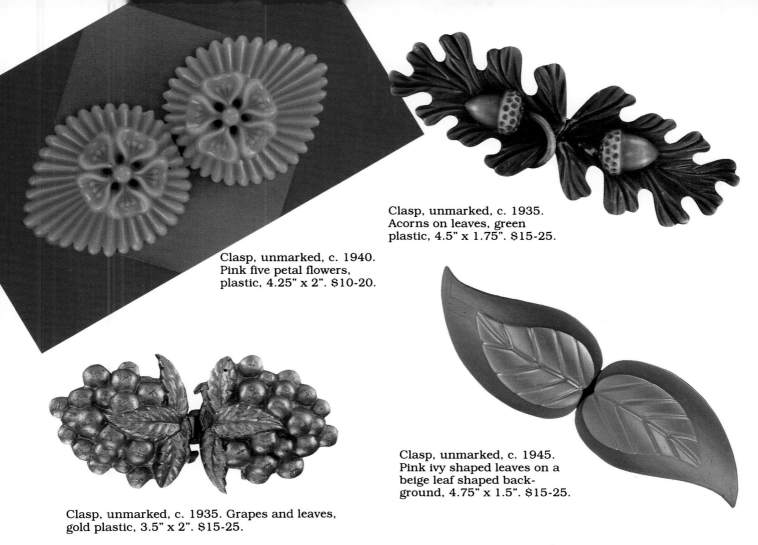

Clasp, unmarked, c. 1940.
Pink five petal flowers,
plastic, 4.25" x 2". $10-20.

Clasp, unmarked, c. 1935.
Acorns on leaves, green
plastic, 4.5" x 1.75". $15-25.

Clasp, unmarked, c. 1945.
Pink ivy shaped leaves on a
beige leaf shaped back-
ground, 4.75" x 1.5". $15-25.

Clasp, unmarked, c. 1935. Grapes and leaves,
gold plastic, 3.5" x 2". $15-25.

Clasp, unmarked, c. 1935.
Brown and green leaves with
silver spots on amber, button
center, 3.25" x 1.25". $15-20.

Clasp, unmarked, c. 1940. Circles of white
snowballs, plastic, 2.25" x 1.25". $10-20.

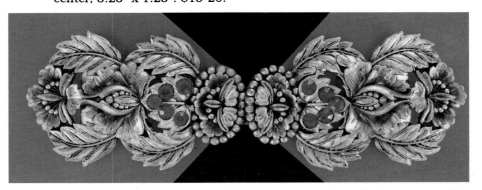

Clasp, unmarked, c. 1935. Silver on plastic with a wild orchid pattern with
red stone trim, 5.25" x 1.75". $30-40.

Buckle, button set, unmarked, c. 1940. Zinnia, green, white, and purple metal petals, with a plastic center on a creme colored plastic base, 4.25" x 2", button, 2" dia.. $35-50.

Buckle, unmarked, on card, marked "BELT SET, Adds style to either Suit or Coat," imitation tortoise, buckle, 3" x 2.75", card is 7.25" x 4.25". $30-40.

Clasp, unmarked, on card marked, "Fashionable Buckles, LeChic," c. 1935. Two leaf shapes in a circle joined by a chain, 1" dia., card is 3" x 4". $5-10.

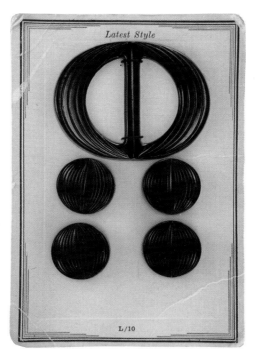

Buckle, unmarked, on card marked "Elegant, Guaranteed Washable, made in USA," c. 1935. Red plastic, circle design with single crossbar, 2.75" dia., card is 2.5" x 3.5". $5-10.

Buckle, button set, unmarked, on card marked "Latest Style L/10," c. 1930. Plastic, brown elliptical pattern, single crossbar on the buckle, 2.25" x 1.75", buttons .8" dia., card is 3.5" x 5.25". $10-20.

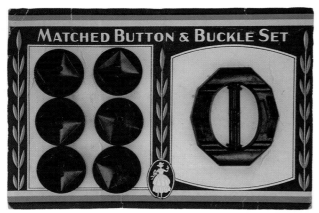

Buckle, button set, unmarked, on card marked "Matched Button & Buckle Set," c. 1940. Black plastic, buckle 1.75" x 1.5", buttons .75" dia. $5-15.

Clasp, unmarked, on card marked "Superior Quality Guaranteed Fast Color made in U.S.A.," c. 1935. Two feather shape black Bakelite piece, connected to a peach colored celluloid disc, .75" x 1.5", card is 3" x 4.25". $10-20.

Buckle, button set, unmarked, on card marked "Majesty Quality Guaranteed Fast Color M," c. 1950. Red plastic scalloped design, buckle is 2.75" x 2.5", buttons, 1"dia., card is 3.75" x 6". $5-15.

Buckle, button set, unmarked, on card marked "LaChic Buckle And Buckle Set Washable Matched for correct style," c. 1945. Orange, buckle 3" x 2", buttons .75" dia., card is 3.5" x 5.25". $5-15.

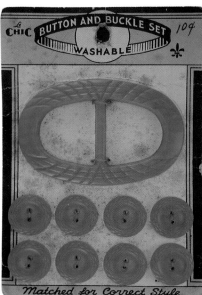

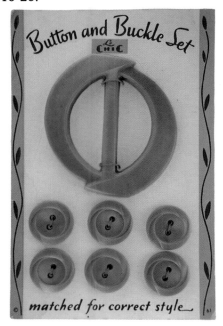

Buckle, button set, unmarked, on card marked "Button and Buckle Set LaChic matched for correct style, " c. 1960. Gray plastic, buckle 2.5" x 2.25", card 3.5" x 5.25". $5-15.

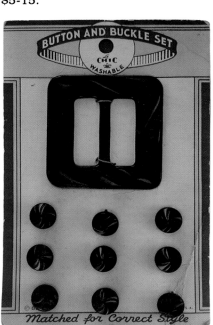

Buckle, button set, unmarked, on card marked "Button And Buckle Set LaChic washable Matched for Correct Style," c. 1945. Brown, buckle 2" sq, buttons .5" dia., card is 3.5" x 5.25". $2-5.

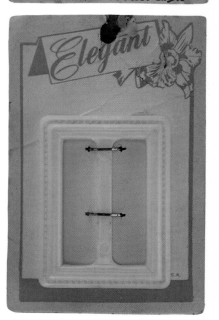

Buckle, unmarked, on card marked "Elegant," c. 1950. Rectangle shaped yellow plastic with single crossbar, 1.5" x 2.25", card is 2.5" x 3.75". $1-5.

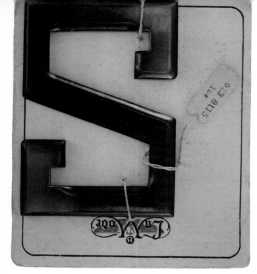

Buckle, unmarked, on card marked "Franken Trimming Co. Inc. 1400 Broadway, New York, N.Y. 10018 style S119 color 344," c. 1960. Green vinyl on a metal base, double crossbar, 2.5" x 1.5", card is 3.25" x 4". $1-5.

Buckle, unmarked, on card marked "LaMode B" tagged, "Halliburton-Abbott Co," c. 1930. S shaped green plastic, 1.75" x 2.75", card is 3" x 3.5". $5-15.

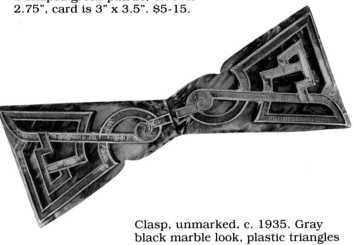

Clasp, unmarked, c. 1935. Gray black marble look, plastic triangles with brass Greek design pattern fastened to the top, 4" x 1.75". $35-50.

Clasp, marked "Greenbaum," c. 1940. Pink roses and leaves with rhinestone trim, 4" x 1.75". $25-30. *Louise Cook collection.*

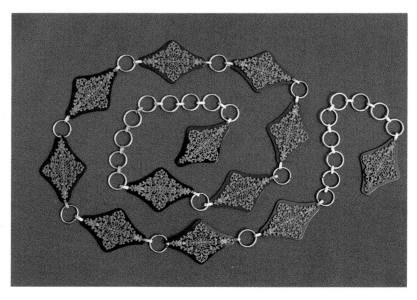

Belt, unmarked, c. 1950. Stamped brass filigree on a black plastic base joined by plated metal rings, 1.5" x 46". $15-20.

Clasp, unmarked, c. 1930. Rust colored Bakelite, large circles in center with continuous small circular motions on each end, 3.25" x 2". $60-75.

Buckle, unmarked, c. 1940. Three green plastic cameos on a brown plastic base, 4.25" x 3". $25-30. *Evelyn Gibbons collection*.

Clasp, unmarked, c. 1925. Green black marble look plastic base, with Egyptian heads on black discs, 5" x 2.5". $40-50.

Buckle, slide, unmarked, c. 1910. Cream color plastic with red overtones, oval shaped, curved, Victorian style, 5" x 3.25". $50-60.

Chapter Four
Buckles Made From Natural Materials

It is only natural that buckles are made from materials such as wood, shell, horn, leather and ivory. All of these can be carved, painted, engraved and decorated with other materials or used as decoration on other materials.

Horn

The term *horn* in buckle making applies to buckles made of both horn and hoof. Horn is a semi-transparent, tough, flexible substance composed of condensed albuminoid substance called keratin. Horn and its allied substance, hoof, are easily reduced to a plastic state by directly applied heat, by boiling in water, or by placing them in a weak solution of alkali. While in a softened condition the material can be bent into any shape or made to adhere to itself. Horn can be dyed almost any color, but buckles made of horn were mostly black or dark brown.

A commercial process of heat molding horn and hoof material was developed in the early 1800s. A Frenchman, Emile Bassot, patented a process for molding horn and hoof material in 1830 and gave great impetus to the industry in France. The British were also major manufacturers of horn products. In preparation, the horn and hoof was split or sawn and flattened. The sheets of prepared material were then scraped, smoothed, polished and dyed. Molding was done by pressing the horn sheets between hot molds or dies. To retain its shape the buckle remained in the mold till cool. Scraps of horn and hoof were powdered, compressed and heated in molds also, so there was no waste.

Clasp, mother of pearl, carved leaf design with scalloped edge, riveted to a brass backplate with faceted cut steels, 1.5" x 2.5". $25-35.

Ivory

Ivory, unlike bone which it resembles, has always been considered a precious material. The elephant tusk is considered to be the true ivory, but commercially, the teeth and tusks of the hippopotamus, walrus, narwhal, and sperm whale are also included. Ivory can be distinguished from imitations by its grain of fine arched or contour lines that intersect. The primary use of ivory is through carving and polishing.

Shell

Buckles have been made from a variety of mollusk shells and are usually referred to as pearl or mother-of-pearl. The use of shell in jewelry and fashion accessories, including buckles, became popular in the eighteenth and nineteenth centuries. American manufacturers began making shell buckles by the late 1890s from clam shells found in rivers. Shells come in shades of

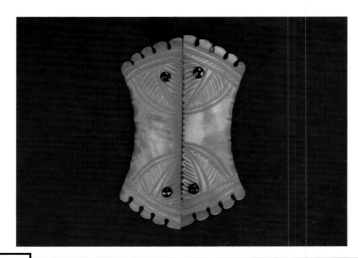

brown, gray, lavender and cream, but fresh-water shells lack the iridescence of shells harvested from salt water.

Shell is a soft material and therefore easy to carve, engrave and polish, which was done almost entirely by hand. Shell, especially pearl, was used as an inlay in many different materials.

Wood

Wood is readily available and easily worked and is a fall back material when others are scarce. During World War II, metal was limited for the jewelry industry and wood was used. Wood was often used in combination with other materials and has been inlaid, carved and painted.

Clasp, blue dyed pearl, cut to shape and pierced ends, riveted to a plated metal hook, 2.5" x 1.25". $10-20.

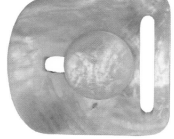

Buckle, button, mother of pearl, pearl is slotted to accommodate the button fastener, slotted to accommodate cloth, 1.75" x 2". $15-25. *Ulta Lowe collection.*

Buckle, mother of pearl, cut to shape and pierced, single closure, trimmed in faceted cut steels, 2" x 1.75". $20-25.

Clasp, abalone shell, cut to shape leaf design, clasp riveted to abalone shell with faceted cut steels, 3.75" x 1.5". $25-35.

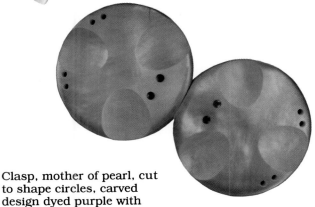

Clasp, mother of pearl, cut to shape circles, carved design dyed purple with metal clasp riveted to shell,

Buckle, mother of pearl, rectangle shape carved design, double closure of brass riveted to shell, 2" x 1.25". $5-15.

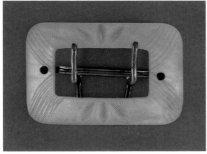

Buckle, slide, mother of pearl, cut to shape shell pierced back, hand carved, single cross bar riveted to the shell, 2.75" x 1.5". $25-30.

Buckle, mother of pearl, cut to shape shell, monogram "S", double slot, 2" x 1.5". $5-10.

Buckle, mother of pearl, cut to shape shell carved top, double closure, brass riveted to shell, 2" x 1.75". $10-15.

Buckle, mother of pearl, cut to shape shell, cat eyed, carved design, trimmed in faceted cut steels, three prong closure, 3" x 1.5". $20-25.

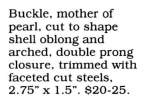

Buckle, mother of pearl, cut to shape shell oblong and arched, double prong closure, trimmed with faceted cut steels, 2.75" x 1.5". $20-25.

Buckle, abalone shell, rectangle shape three prong closure, 3" x 2.25". $10-15.

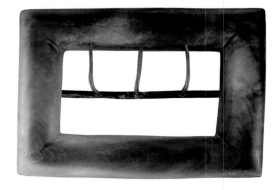

Buckle, mother of pearl, cut to shape shell with double prong closure mounted at opposing corners, 2"sq.. $10-15.

Clasp, mother of pearl, rectangle shaped, stamped brass, with prong set pearl, 2.75" x 1". $20-30.

Buckle, mother of pearl, cut to shape slotted shell, with three prong closure, riveted to the shell with faceted cut steels, 3" x 1.25". $10-15.

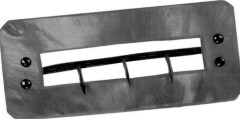

Buckle, mother of pearl, arched cut to shape shell, with double prong closure, 3" x 2". $5-10.

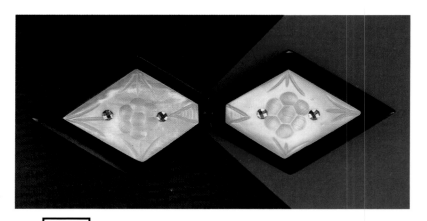

Clasp, red tint celluloid roses on a shell back, 2.75" x 1.25". $25-35.

Clasp, cut to shape carved pearl, riveted to a bakelite base with faceted cut steels, 5" x 1.75". $35-50.

Buckle, mother of pearl, cut to shape, carved and pierced, shape of a lyre, single prong closure, 1.75" x 2.75". $35-45.

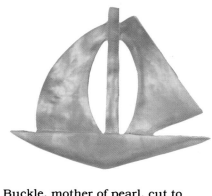

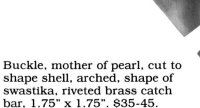

Buckle, mother of pearl, cut to shape shell, arched, shape of swastika, riveted brass catch bar, 1.75" x 1.75". $35-45.

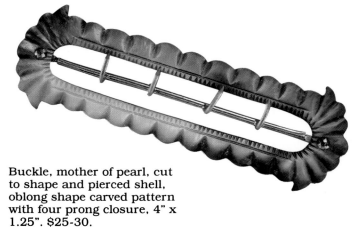

Buckle, mother of pearl, cut to shape and pierced shell, shape of sailboat, 2.5" x 2". $25-35.

Buckle, mother of pearl, cut to shape and pierced shell, rectangle shape with carved waffle pattern, three prong closure, 1.75" x 1.25". $20-25.

Buckle, mother of pearl, cut to shape and pierced shell, oblong shape carved pattern with four prong closure, 4" x 1.25". $25-30.

Clasp, marked "T.S.," c. 1880. Gold flowers and birds on pearl, sterling on brass, 3.25" x 2.25". $300-350.

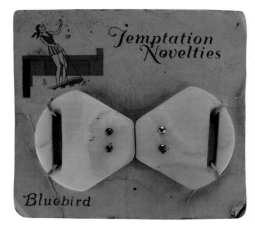

Clasp, unmarked, on card marked "Temptation Novelties Bluebird," c. 1945. Pearl, cut to shape, 3" x 1.5", card is 3.25" x 3". $15-20.

Clasp, unmarked, on card marked "Superior finish," c. 1930. Pearl, cut to shape, 1.25" x .5", card is 2.8" x 2.25". $10-20.

Buckle, unmarked, on card marked "Lady Washington Pearls," c. 1930. Pearl, dyed yellow cut to shape single crossbar, 2.5" x 1.75", card is 3.25" x 3". $15-20.

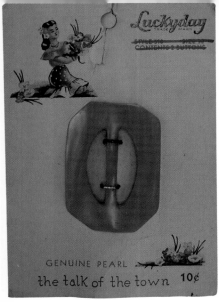

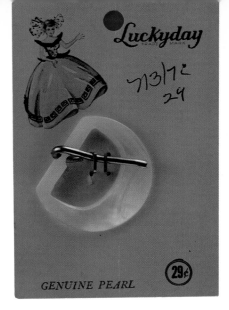

Buckle, unmarked, on card marked "Luckyday trade mark Genuine Pearl the talk of the town," c. 1935. Pearl, dyed red cut to shape single crossbar, 1.25" x 1.75", card is 3" x 4.25". $15-25.

Buckle, unmarked, on card marked "Luckyday trade mark Genuine pearl," c. 1940. Pearl, cut to shape with single metal closure prong, 1.5" x 1.25", card is 2.5" x 3.75". $5-15.

Buckle, unmarked, on card marked "Lansing Pearls Washable A Great Name In Buttons," c. 1940. Pearl, natural color cut to shape single crossbar, 1" x 1.5", card is 2.5" x 3.5". $10-20.

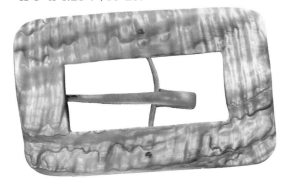

Clasp, unmarked, c. 1900. Victorian lady wearing a hat, brass on pearl, on a white metal base, 3" x 1.25". $35-45. *Evelyn Gibbons collection.*

Buckle, unmarked, c. 1900. Rectangle, alabaster shell with single closure, 3" x 2". $20-30. *Connie Fitzner collection.*

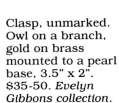

Clasp, unmarked. Owl on a branch, gold on brass mounted to a pearl base, 3.5" x 2". $35-50. *Evelyn Gibbons collection.*

Buckle, unmarked. Pearl, horseshoe shape with faceted cut steel and double prong closure, 2.5" x 3". $25-35. *Annie Frazier collection.*

Clasp, unmarked. Man and woman sitting on fence, gold wash stamped brass on pearl base, ball and chain trim, 4" x 2". $35-50. *Annie Frazier collection.*

Clasp, unmarked, c. 1955. Wood, rectangle shaped, carved male and female snow skier, 4.25" x 1.75". $35-40.

Buckle, unmarked, c. 1960. Round, pierced back, single bar, coconut material, 2.25" dia.. $5-10.

Buckle, unmarked, c. 1960. Wood rectangle with pierced back and single wood closure prong, 2.25" x 2". $20-25.

Buckle, slide, unmarked, c. 1950-1970. Square shape, rounded corners with two slots at cross corners, 1.75" sq.. $5.

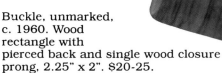

Buckle, unmarked, c. 1950. Pressed wood rectangle, sailboat design with single bar, rope design edge, 3" x 2.5". $20-25.

Buckle, unmarked, c. 1950. Wood, carved leaf pattern imitation tortoise closure prong, 3" dia.. $15-20.

Buckle, unmarked, c. 1950. Carved wood circle, metal bar with single wood closure, 4" dia.. $20-25.

Buckle, unmarked, c. 1940. Carved wood rectangle with single plated metal closure, 2.75" x 2.5". $15-25.

Clasp, marked "Made in Czecho-Slovakia Registered," c. 1950. Rectangle shaped with shoelace pattern, gray color, 3.5" x 2". $25-35.

Buckle, unmarked, c. 1950. Pressed wood rectangle, flower and leaf design, single cross bar, 2.75" x 2.5". $20-25.

Buckle, unmarked, c. 1960. Round wood circle with green button plastic trims recessed, single metal cross bar. Note, missing closure prong, 2.75" dia.. $10-20.

Buckle, unmarked, c. 1950. Carved wood circle with cerated edge, triangle shape crossbar with imitation tortoise closure prong, 3" dia.. $15-20.

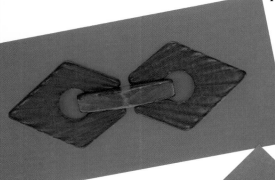

Clasp, marked "Made in Czechoslovakia Registered," c. 1950. Carved wood triangles, joined by a wooden bar on metal pins, purple color, 3" x 1.25". $20-25.

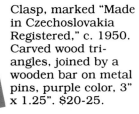

Buckle, unmarked, c. 1950. Wood square, recessed at crossed corners with two slots, 1.75" sq.. $10-20.

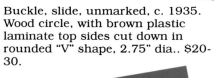

Buckle, slide, unmarked, c. 1935. Wood circle, with brown plastic laminate top sides cut down in rounded "V" shape, 2.75" dia.. $20-30.

Buckle, unmarked, c. 1950. Round, carved wood circle with five petal flower design, single crossbar, 2.5" dia.. $10-20.

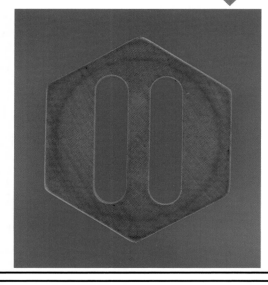

Buckle, unmarked, c. 1960. Six sided, wood with two slots, 2.25" x 2.75". $5-10.

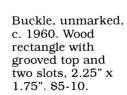

Buckle, unmarked, c. 1960. Wood rectangle with grooved top and two slots, 2.25" x 1.75". $5-10.

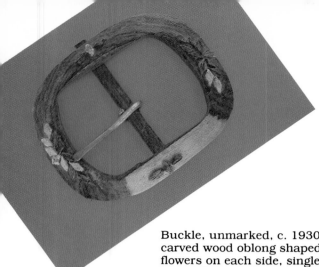

Buckle, unmarked, c. 1935. Hand carved, wood flowers on each corner, single wood bar and plastic closure prong, 3" x 2.75". $30-40. *Clare Hatten collection.*

Buckle, unmarked, c. 1930. Hand carved wood oblong shaped, carved flowers on each side, single cross bar and metal closure, 3.5" x 2.75". $35-40. *Clare Hatten collection.*

Buckle, unmarked, on card marked "LaMode," c. 1935. Wood with carved top blue enamel trim, single metal closure prong, 2.5" x 1.75", card is 3" x 3.5". $10-20.

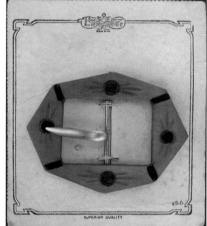

Buckle, unmarked, on card marked "LaMode Superior quality," c. 1935. Wood with carved top, dyed red with black trim, single metal closure prong, 2.5" x 2", card is 3" x 3.5". $10-20.

Buckle, unmarked, on card marked "LaChic,"c. 1940. Wood with waffle pattern top, single cross bar, 2" x 1.75", card is 3" x 2.25". $10-20.

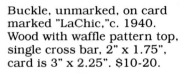

Buckle, unmarked, on card marked "Ultra Kraft 1954," c. 1955. Round shape, with rope cross pattern, single cross bar, 3" dia., card is 3.5" x 4.25". $10-20.

Belt, unmarked, c. 1950. Carved coconut shell joined by metal loops, 1.5" x 34". $15-25.

Set, buckle and buttons, unmarked, c. 1930. Burl wood buckle and six buttons, buckle is 2.5" dia., buttons 1" dia.. $40-50. *Ulta Lowe collection*.

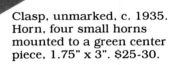

Clasp, unmarked, c. 1935. Horn, four small horns mounted to a green center piece, 1.75" x 3". $25-30.

Clasp, marked "7," c. 1850-1900. Hickory nut and leaf pattern, black dyed pressed horn, 2.5" x 2.25". $50-75.

Clasp, unmarked, c. 1850-1900. Spray of flowers in an oval, black dyed pressed horn, 3" x 2.25". $50-75.

Clasp, unmarked, c. 1850-1900. Grape leaves, grapes and vines in an oval, black dyed pressed horn, 2.5" x 2". $50-75.

Clasp, unmarked, c. 1850-1900. Sunflowers and leaves mounted on "D" shaped base, black dyed pressed horn, 3" x 2". $50-75.

Clasp, unmarked, c. 1900. Black dyed pressed horn, figure of a woman with water jug standing in water, 3.5"x 2.25". $75-100.

Clasp, unmarked, c. 1850-1900. Fern leaf pattern, black dyed pressed horn, 2.5" x 2". $50-75.

Clasp, unmarked, c. 1850-1900. Grapes, leaves, and vines in a "D" shape, black dyed pressed horn, 2.25" x 2". $50-75.

Clasp for fur stole, unmarked, c. 1925. Brown, crocheted, snaps with imitation tortoise links, 7" x .75". $25-30.

Buckle, unmarked, c. 1920. Diamond shape, eight polished agate stones bezel set in a gold washed brass base, single prong closure, 4" x 2". $45-55.

Clasp, marked "China," c. 1900. Four polished Malachite stones, set in a silver on brass base, trimmed with beaded rolled wire, 3.75" x 1.25". $150-200.

Chapter Five
Shoe Buckles

Shoe buckles have been in and out of vogue from as early as the fourteenth century. They were common in England in the early 1500s, but by the end of the century they were being replaced by rosettes and ribbon ties. Around 1660 shoe buckles once again gained in popularity, first in Italy and France then in England during the reign of Charles II. The fashion soon passed to America where wealthy colonists followed the European fashion trends. By 1685, the buckle was the dominate fastener for shoes. When first introduced buckles were small and set high on the instep, and gradually they became larger and more impressive. It was the men who first wore shoe buckles, but during this time period references to women's shoes having buckles can be found.

In Birmingham, England, the craft of buckle-making started in the late seventeenth century and was firmly established by the beginning of the eighteenth century. It is estimated that 2,500,000 pairs of buckles were manufactured there annually. Shoe buckles were often ornately fashioned from gold, silver, copper, brass, pewter and iron. They were also engraved, gilded, enameled or set with stones.

Shoe buckles became a status symbol with noblemen wearing silver buckles set with diamonds. The gentry wore silver buckles on Sundays and gilded buckles for everyday wear.

In the 1770s, the fashion changed again and the shoestring once more was the dominating shoe fastener, much to the dismay of the buckle manufacturers. In an attempt to revive the falling fashion in America, it is said that tickets to exclusive places of entertainment were printed with the following: "Gentlemen with shoe-strings not admitted." But the shoe buckle fell from grace.

About 100 years later, in the 1870s, the shoe buckle was revived for a short time, but it wasn't until the late nineteenth century and early twentieth century that the shoe buckle once again dominated fashion. A change had transpired—the shoe buckle passed from men's fashion to women's.

In the 1900s, the shoe buckle was worn on all types of shoes, from street shoes to evening shoes. Cut-steel buckles with their jewel-like qualities added elegance to any type shoe.

Shoe buckle, marked "Sterling Top F&Co Silverite F&Co," c. 1900. Rhinestones set in silver, with a green enamel border, 1.25" x 1". $35-50.

Shoe buckle, marked "Sterling," c. 1900. Single buckle, silver on brass, curved with etched pattern, 2" x 1.75". $35-40.

Shoe buckle pair, marked "France Holfast Pat. App For," c. 1850-1910. Faceted cut steels on a curved brass base, three petal flower at each corner with a diamond shape in the middle, 2" x 1.75". $50-75.

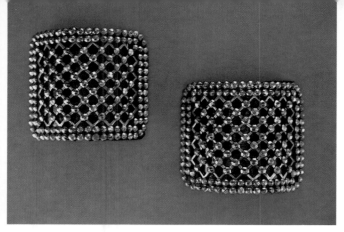

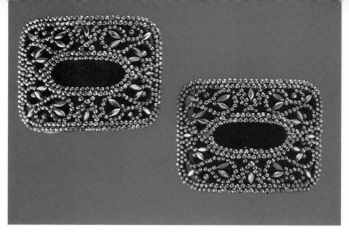

Shoe buckle pair, marked "Made in France ARLE," c. 1850-1910. Faceted cut steels on a curved brass base, criss cross pattern with double row of steels on border, 2" x 1.75". $50-75.

Shoe buckle pair, marked "France," c. 1850-1910. Faceted cut steels on a brass base, two petal flower pattern, oval opening in center, 2.5" x 1.75". $50-75.

Shoe buckle pair, marked "HOLD-TH Pat.Pend," c. 1850-1910. Faceted cut steels on a brass base, three petal flowers in the corners, oval opening in the center, 2.25" x 1.75". $50-75.

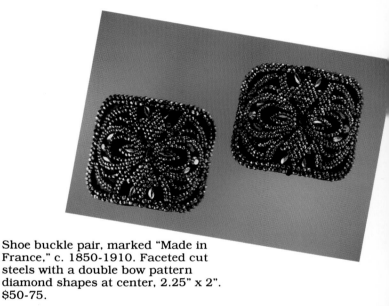

Shoe buckle pair, marked "Made in France," c. 1850-1910. Faceted cut steels with a double bow pattern diamond shapes at center, 2.25" x 2". $50-75.

Shoe buckle pair, marked "France," c. 1850-1910. Faceted cut steels on a brass base, eight petal flower of cut steels with double row border, 2.25" x 2". $50-75.

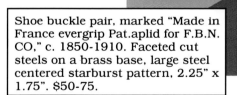

Shoe buckle pair, marked "Made in France evergrip Pat.aplid for F.B.N. CO," c. 1850-1910. Faceted cut steels on a brass base, large steel centered starburst pattern, 2.25" x 1.75". $50-75.

Shoe buckle pair, marked "Made in France," c. 1850-1910. Plated stamped brass oblong shape, scalloped shaped center riveted to a brass base, 2.25" x 1.75". $25-40.

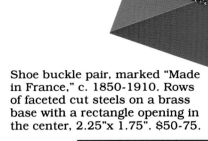

Shoe buckle pair, marked "France," c. 1850-1910. Rows of faceted cut steels, with oval opening in the center on a brass base, 2.25" x 1.5". $50-75.

Shoe buckle pair, marked "Made in France," c. 1850-1910. Rows of faceted cut steels on a brass base with a rectangle opening in the center, 2.25"x 1.75". $50-75.

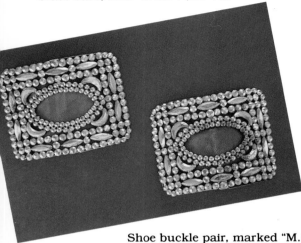

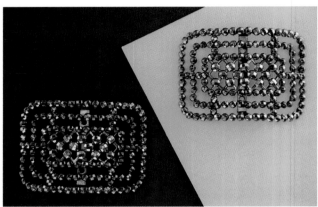

Shoe buckle pair, marked "M.G. France," c. 1850-1910. Oxidized faceted cut steels, double row of small steels forming a oval in the center with quarter moon shapes at each corner, 2.25" x 1.75". $50-75.

Shoe buckle pair, marked "France," c. 1850-1910. Rows of faceted cut steels in rectangle shapes, center rectangle with diamond shaped pattern, 2.25" x 1.75". $50-75.

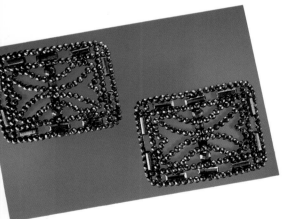

Shoe buckle pair, marked "France," c. 1850-1910. Faceted cut steels on a brass base, row of rectangle steels double heart pattern in the center, 2.25" x 1.75". $50-75.

Shoe buckle pair, unmarked, c. 1850-1910. Oval shape, oval center opening with scalloped rows between outer and inner row, 2.5" x 1.5". $40-60.

Shoe buckle pair, marked "France," c. 1850-1910. Faceted cut steels with diamond shape center, 2" x 1.5". $50-75.

Shoe buckle pair, front and back, marked "LW Paris," c. 1850-1910. Oxidized faceted cut steels on a brass base, floral pattern, center star, 2.25" x 1.75". $50-75.

Shoe buckle pair, unmarked, c. 1920. Imitation cut steel, gold paint, cast base metal rectangle shaped, 2.25" x 1.5". $15-25.

Shoe buckle pair, un-marked, c. 1940. Silver luster, black glass beads in a winged pattern with three smoked gray glass beads in the center, 2.5" x .75". $15-25.

Shoe buckle pair, unmarked, c. 1900. Oxidized, stamped brass pattern, center opening bow shaped, 2.25" x 1.75". $15-25.

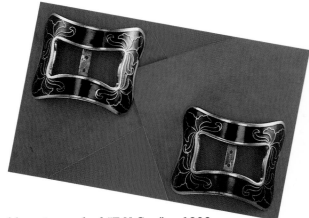

Shoe buckle pair, unmarked, c. 1935. Oxidized stamped brass, flowing ribbon pattern, 2.5" x 2". $15-25.

Shoe buckle pair, marked "F.N.Co.," c. 1900. Silver on brass cloisonné floral pattern, black enamel, 2" x 1.75". $50-75.

Shoe buckle pair, un-marked, c. 1935. Oxi-dized, cast pattern on a brass oval with a green emerald cut rhinestone, 2" x 1.5". $25-50.

Shoe buckle pair, un-marked, c. 1920. Silver on brass rectangles, stamped and etched pattern, prong set red cabochons, 2" x 1". $25-50.

Shoe buckle pair, unmarked, c. 1940. Silver on cast base metal pavé set rhinestones, foliage pattern, 1.5" x 1". $25-50.

Shoe buckle pair, unmarked, c. 1940. Bow shape, silver on base metal felt bows, 2.25" x 1.25". $25-50.

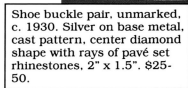

Shoe buckle pair, unmarked, c. 1920. Silver on brass, layered stamped brass patterns, 2.25" x 1.75". $35-50.

Shoe buckle pair, unmarked, c. 1930. Silver on base metal, cast pattern, center diamond shape with rays of pavé set rhinestones, 2" x 1.5". $25-50.

Shoe buckle pair, unmarked, c. 1950. Bow shaped, prong set rhinestones in a plated base, 2" x 1". $20-40.

Shoe buckle pair, marked "c MUSI," c. 1950. Rows of prong set rhinestones in a gold enamel base, 2.25" x 1.25". $20-40.

Shoe buckle pair, marked "Silverite," c. 1925. Pavé set rhinestones in a silver on base metal, cast base, 1.75" x 1.25". $25-50.

Shoe buckle pair, unmarked, c. 1930. Black plastic, round pattern in white enamel with a ring of pavé set rhinestones, 2.25" x 2". $15-20.

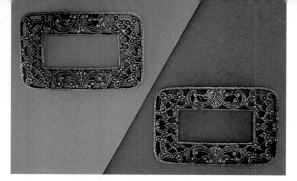

Shoe buckle pair, marked "c MUSI," c. 1930. Oxidized cast base metal, floral pattern, 2.25" x 1.5". $10-15.

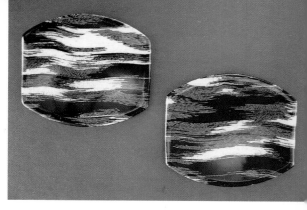

Shoe buckle pair, unmarked, c. 1935. Black, white, and gray blend plastic, 2.25" x 2". $10-15.

Shoe buckle pair, unmarked, c. 1950. Double row of prong set rhinestones in plated metal base, 2" x .3". $10-15.

Shoe buckles, marked, c. 1930. *Top*: Marked "TK," rectangle shaped, pavé set rhinestones in a cast white metal base, 1.25" x .75". $5-10. *Middle*: Marked "Nov-E-Line," oval shaped, pavé set rhinestones in cast white metal base, 1.75" x 1.25". $5-10. *Bottom*: Marked, rectangle shaped, pavé set rhinestones in a white metal base, diamond shape center in a floral pattern, 2.25" x 1.75". $10-15.

Shoe buckles, unmarked, c. 1930. Top: Oval shaped, layered celluloid, 2" x 1.5". $5-10. Bottom: Rectangle shaped, celluloid with etched and painted floral pattern, 2" x 1.5". $10-15.

Shoe buckle, unmarked, c. 1935. Square, oxidized filigree border, grape vine, leaves, and grapes surrounding a large green glass cabochon, 1.75" sq.. $15-25.

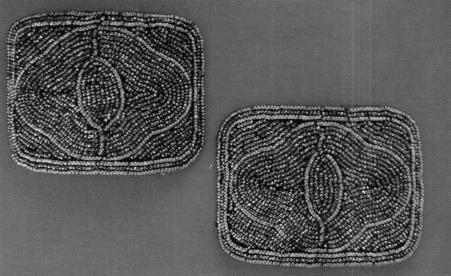

Shoe buckle, unmarked, c. 1930.
Imitation carnelian glass stone, prong
set in an oval brass base, 1.25" x 1.75".
$15-25.

Shoe buckle pair, marked "Made in
France," c. 1850-1910. Imitation cut steel,
rows of tiny glass beads, 2.5" x 2". $50-75.

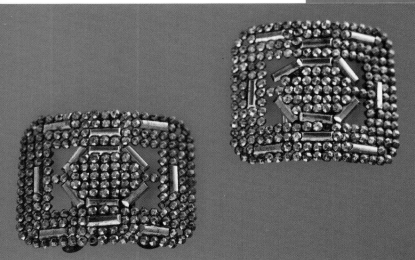

Shoe buckle pair, marked
"Made in France," c. 1850-
1910. Faceted cut steels,
square design, 2" x 1.75". $50-
65.

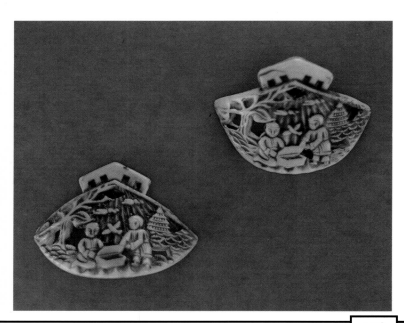

Shoe buckle pair, marked "France," c. 1850-1910.
Faceted cut steels, geometric design, 2.25" x 1.75".
$50-65.

Shoe buckle pair, unmarked, c. 1900.
Oriental scene in Celluloid, 2" x 1.5".
$25-50.

Clasp, unmarked, c. 1910. Carved shell cameo set in a brass base, mounted on an ornate back, 4" x 3". $150-200.

Chapter Six
Unique and Unusual Buckles

This chapter is devoted to a selected number of fine buckles. They have been chosen for their uniqueness and beauty.

Clasp, marked, "Made in Italy," c. 1920. Mosaic tile, bouquet of flowers in a blue green oval, surrounded by white fan scallops, set in an octagon shaped brass base, 2" x 1.25". $350-500. Rare.

Buckle, marked, "IWPD 27," c. 1850-1900. A historical commemorative buckle of Lord Palmerston, Henry John Temple. Stamped brass, Heads of Lord Palmerston, shows date of birth date of death, displayed on card with news article and short history, 1.75" x 2.75". *Evelyn Gibbons collection.*

Clasp, unmarked, c.1920. Mosaic tile, multi-color flower pattern, cut to shape, gold wash brass base, 2.25" x 1.75". $300-500. Rare.

Buckle, marked, c. 1900. Satsuma. Irises, enamel on ceramic, gold trim in a silver on brass base, 1.5" dia. $90-125.

Belt, marked, "DEPOSE, O.G.," c. 1920. Egyptian, seventeen gold wash, stamped brass filigree squares with champleve enamel, Egyptian figures, joined by brass links. Buckle, gold washed filigree backplate with champleve Egyptian enameled heads, and a center mounted medallion, buckle is 3.5" x 1.75". Overall length 29.5". $500-650.

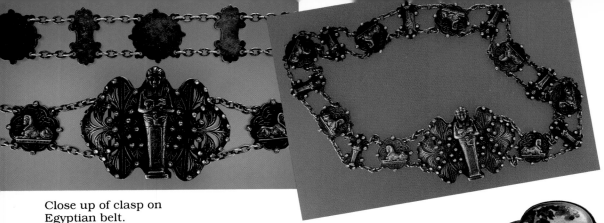

Close up of clasp on Egyptian belt.

Belt, unmarked, c. 1920. Egyptian, Pharaoh and sphinx panels with amber rhinestone trim, joined by metal link chain, with large clasp of a Pharaoh with a feather fan background with rhinestone trim, overall length 28", clasp is 3.5" x 2.5". $500-650.

Clasp, marked, c. 1900. Satsuma, oriental scene of house by a lake, design outlined in gold, set in a gold wash brass base, 3.25" x 2". $275-325.

Clasp, marked, "C," c. 1920. Gold washed, cast base metal with picture of ice skaters, decal on plastic, with rhinestone trim, 2.75" x 1.75". $20-30.

Clasp, marked, "Brevetté, c. 1910. Victorian style, stamped brass leaves around a center filigree housing a gold trembler, highlighting a large, faceted, amber colored, glass jewel, 5.5" x 2". $250-300. Rare. *Annie Frazier collection*.

Clasp, marked, "C," c. 1920. Gold washed, cast base metal with picture of man and woman in garden, decal on plastic, with rhinestone trim, 2.75" x 1.75". $20-30.

Clasp, unmarked, c. 1900. Gold washed, stamped brass pattern of flowers and leaves, bezel set glass oval with glass cameo, 3" x 2". $35-40.

Clasp, unmarked, c. 1890. Heart shape circle of gold washed, vines, leaves, and flowers surrounding a handpainted portrait on ivory, under glass, 3.75" x 2.5". $125-150. *Annie Frazier collection*.

Buckle, unmarked, c. 1900. Carved ivory, flowers and foliage, 2.5" x 1.75". $150-200.

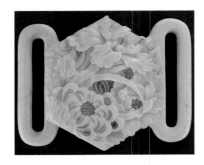

Display tray, rhinestone shoe buckles. A collage of pairs and single shoe buckles.

Display tray, six metal buckles and clasps with unusual fastening devices.

Chapter Seven
Display and Competition

Serious and casual collectors will want a way to enjoy their finds. One of the most common ways is to mount the buckles on non acidic board with plastic coated wire, such as telephone wire. Telephone wire will not damage the buckle in most cases and will not corrode. Do not use pipe cleaners as they will rust and corrode if they get wet, which will then be transferred to the buckle. The board can be obtained through most any of the button clubs in your area.

Buckles can be displayed by material, theme, or by competition requirements and is only limited by one's imagination. Once the buckles are mounted they can be put in wood frames with glass fronts and hung on the wall.

Old type-setting cabinets, glass topped display cases, or any enclosed cabinet can be used to store and display buckle collections while protecting them from sunlight, dust, and dirt. Carded buckles can also be stored in plastic bins with sealable lids in a cool, dry place.

Below are several examples of carded buckles for display.

Display tray, eight faceted cut steel clasps, with various designs and trims.

Display tray, five cape clasps, metal with plastic and glass trims, matching button.

Display tray, made up for a spring show, theme "Spring Flowers." Six pair, clasps, all metal. Created just for the fun of it! A participation ribbon was presented to each person entering trays.

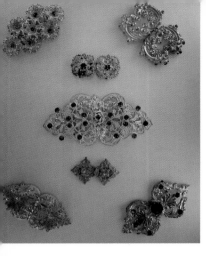

Display tray, seven gold washed stamped brass clasps with various prong set rhinestones.

Display tray, four metal clasps mounted vertically.

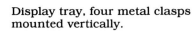

Display card. Eight clasps of plastic flowers mounted for display with blue flower decorations.

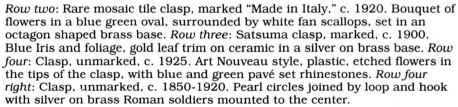

Open competition tray, 1995 Blue Ribbon, National button show, Orlando, Florida, Division IV, Section 7, Class: 30. Buckles assorted, (six pairs per card, any type fastening device). *Left to right, top to bottom. Top left*: Cloisonné butter-fly, unmarked, c. 1920. Enamel on a brass groundplate. *Top right*: Clasp, marked, c. 1900. Oval shape, silver on brass filigree with four bezel set, green cabochons around an imitation sword. *Row two*: Rare mosaic tile clasp, marked "Made in Italy," c. 1920. Bouquet of flowers in a blue green oval, surrounded by white fan scallops, set in an octagon shaped brass base. *Row three*: Satsuma clasp, marked, c. 1900. Blue Iris and foliage, gold leaf trim on ceramic in a silver on brass base. *Row four*: Clasp, unmarked, c. 1925. Art Nouveau style, plastic, etched flowers in the tips of the clasp, with blue and green pavé set rhinestones. *Row four right*: Clasp, unmarked, c. 1850-1920. Pearl circles joined by loop and hook with silver on brass Roman soldiers mounted to the center.

Open competition tray, Division IV, Section 7, Class: 30. Buckles assorted, six pair per card, (any type fastening device). *Row one*: Horseshoe shaped clasp, gold washed plastic with pavé set rhinestones. *Row two: Left*:Cut to shape and polished prong set turquoise stones in a silver on white metal base, with pavé set rhinestones. *Right*: Oriental clasp, red cinnabar, oriental characters, flowers and foliage in a brass base. *Row three*: White roses and foliage in a shaped and formed green plastic. *Row four: Left*: blue beads sewn to a brass base with a faceted blue gem in the center. *Right*: Ibis heads, gold washed cast brass. *Courtesy of Mabel Clark.*

Competition tray, Division IV, Section 7, Class 30. Buckles assorted, (six pair per card, any type fastening device). *Top left*: Small two piece enamel. *Top right*: Cast, white metal, flowers with rainbow color stones. *Middle left*: Black Bakelite, Daffodil flowers. *Middle right*: Heart shaped pressed, faceted, black glass bordered by prong set rhinestones. *Bottom left*: Stamped brass circle, oriental design. *Bottom right*: Celluloid, tan with silver stripes. *Courtesy of Ulta Lowe.*

Open competition or display tray, Division IV, Section 7, class: 30. Buckles assorted (6 pairs per card, any type fastening device). *Left to right, top to Bottom: Top left*: Clasp, unmarked, c. 1900. Gold washed brass lion heads mounted to a wood back, in a brass ring with faceted cut steel trim, joined by hook and eye. *Top right*: Clasp, unmarked, c. 1900. Cast brass horses with faceted cut steel trim on a stamped brass base. *Row two*: Clasp, unmarked, c. 1910. Brass scarabs with faceted cut steel trim on a Bakelite base. *Row three left*: Clasp, unmarked, c. 1920. Silver on brass, eagle head with flowers and foliage. *Row three right*: Clasp, marked "Czechoslo-vakia," c. 1925. Foil under glass, white swans and yellow flowers prong set in a brass base. *Row four*: Clasp, unmarked, c. 1950. White plastic elephants.

While displaying buckles in your home is very satisfying, there are other ways to share your collection and to gain knowledge. Most states have a Button Society and small clubs are formed by individuals in different areas of the state. Twice a year the clubs get together for a display theme, a workshop, or a competition. The themes can range from "Spring Flowers", to "Fantastic Fasteners," two of the Michigan Button Societies' most recent themes. Workshops present themes on material, history, competition and many other interesting topics. Rules for competition are established by the National Button Society, and published in the OFFICIAL NBS CLASSIFICATION SYSTEM and updated annually.

Open competition tray, Division IV, Section 7, Class: 30. Buckles assorted, (6 pairs per card, any type fastening device). *Top to bottom, left to right*: Egyptian heads, celluloid. *Row two*: Carved pearl wings. *Row three*: Green and white baked enamel. *Row four left*: Bakelite base with brass filigree circles. *Center*: Faceted cut steel butterfly. *Right*: Imitation amber.

Open competition or display tray, Division IV, Section 7, class: 31. Buckles assorted (6 pairs per card, centered button shanks only). *Left to right, top to bottom: Row one left*: Clasp, unmarked, c. 1900. Stamped brass dragon with an ornate border, joined by hook and eye. *Right*: Clasp, unmarked, c. 1920. MADAME CHRYSANTHEME. One piece brass, stamped and pierced with a steel inset on the fan. *Row two left*: Clasp, unmarked, c. 1900. Pressed black glass with a flower design. *Right*: Clasp, unmarked, c. 1900. Brass grapes and leaves on a fence, fastened to a steel back with a faceted cut steel, joined by a hook and eye with a ball and chain trim. *Row three left*: Clasp, unmarked, c. 1900. Cut steel disc with a sunburst center and ornate trim, joined by hook and eye with ball and chain trim. *Right*: Clasp, unmarked, c. 1900. Leather discs with raised design and cut steel trims.

OPPOSITE: Special awards competition tray, Division IV, (97) Section 7, Class 30, 6 pairs. Buckles specialized to enamels. *Top to bottom, left to right*: Gold, red, and violet, roses with foliage, with violet, blue, and white background, cut to shape groundplate, design in champlevé and basse-taille enamel. *Top right*: Sunburst pattern, cut to shape and pierced groundplate, champlevé enameling with bezel set imitation jade at centers of sunburst and oblong glass at clasp center, blue, white, and green colors. *Row two*: Cloisonné butterfly, exquisite rare piece. Green, black, brown, gold, and silver colors in a guilt base. *Row three*: Russian style, orthodox design patterns, fastens with sword, red, white, green, blue, and yellow enamel on a cut to shape groundplate, design in champlevé. *Row four left*: Yellow Trillium petals with a blue green background, green and red foliage, outlined in blue. Cut to shape champlevé groundplate, basse-taille enamel. *Row four right*: Tulip shape pattern and outline, cut to shape and pierced, gilt groundplate, champlevé enameling with faceted cut steels trim, blue, red, green, and yellow colors.

Special awards competition tray, Division IV, (98) Section 7, Class 32, 12 any. One piece buckles (meaning you do not need 2 separate pieces). May have other parts such as a tongue. Assorted materials. *Top to bottom, left to right*: Satsuma. Irises, enamel on ceramic, gold trim in a silver on brass base. *Middle*: Diamond shaped, eight polished agate stones bezel set in a gold washed brass base, single prong closure. *Right*: Clear glass buckle, with gold washed stamped brass filigree on four sides with rhinestone trim, single closure prong. *Row two*: Stamped and tinted celluloid, Art Nouveau, figure of woman with roses in her hair, prong set in a gold washed brass base. *Middle*: Oval shaped, gold washed pierced backplate with brass flies and beetles, double prong closure. *Right*: Oblong shaped buckle with crescents on each end topped with small flowers and bezel set green cabochons, opposite sides are filled with an emerald green colored slag glass bezel set in the brass base. *Row three*: Mother of pearl, cut to shape, arched, shape of swastika, riveted brass catch bar. *Right*: Apple and leaf stem shaped rhinestone, prong set clear and red stones set in brass. *Row four*: Rectangle shaped, gold washed stamped brass single closure, fancy feather design with roman coins top and bottom centered, three prong set rhinestones on each end. *Middle*: Circle of paisley shapes highlighted with red and green rhinestones and tiny faceted cut steels riveted to a metal base. *Right*: Clear Lucite with red roses and leaves recessed in the Lucite. *Row five*: Two Cherubim's with roses and foliage, stamped brass.

Special awards competition tray, Division IV, (99) Section 7, Class 32, 6 buckles and 6 buttons. Specialized to 6 buckles, one piece or two piece, and 6 buttons which match and are part of a set. *Top to bottom. Left*: Cape clasp, Gibson girl in brass on a Bakelite base joined by three brass loops. *Right*: Clasp, Bakelite, beige circle on an orange circle. *Row two left*: Buckle, Zinnia, green, white, and purple metal petals with a plastic center on a cream colored plastic base. *Right*: Clasp, white enamel on stamped brass filigree, multi-colored pressed glass beads wired to the base. *Row three left*: Clasp, bird in flight holding branch in beak, stamped tinted brass on wood background, on a brass rimmed base. *Right*: Clasp, stamped brass rippled filigree circles with a circle of prong set multi-colored stones and a large bezel set amber stone at center.

Competition at the state level is determined by the state officers elected by the members. Buckle competition, unfortunately, is not always scheduled. But you can always submit a theme tray to stay active. Or if enough people become active in buckle collecting then a competition will be scheduled at each event.

Applications to compete are available through the state society in which you belong. You must belong to compete.

Open Competition for buckles is listed in the NBS classification system under Division IV, specialties, Section 7 - BUCKLES

Class:

30. Buckles assorted (6 pairs per card, any type fastening device)

31. Buckles assorted (6 pairs per card, centered button shanks only)

32. Buckles specialized

As a member of the National Button society you are eligible to compete on a national level. In the February issue of the *National Button Bulletin* awards for the current year are listed. The May issue of the *National Button Bulletin* has an application for the tray entry form and tray slips for each award you will be competing for. Complete instructions on how and where to send your entries is included. Experienced members of your local button club are more than willing to help prepare you for your first competition.

Proper preparation for competition can result in the thrill of the coveted Blue Ribbon, or in the satisfaction in knowing you did your best. Either way go for it, and happy buckling.

Chapter Eight
Cleaning Buckles

Before starting to clean, it is best to know as much about the piece as possible. Some buckles are very delicate and require special handling, others will stand real abuse. Many fine buckles are found in dirty boxes at flea markets and will have all manner of dirt on them. There are not any set rules for cleaning buckles. What is written here is meant to be used as a guide, caution must always be exercised, even after you feel you have adequate experience in identifying materials.

For the serious collector, the following is a list of items that will aid you in cleaning your buckles, as your confidence grows you will probably add to the list.

One soft and one stiff bristled brush. Toothbrush or jewelers brushes.

Soft cloths and Turkish towels

Toothpicks or old dental tool (found at flea markets)

Jewelry cleaning solution

Eye loop or magnifying glass

Wide mouth glass jar

Small needle nose pliers

Glue

Pencil eraser

ened brush can be used to loosen it, or with severe dirt a tooth pick or metal pick can be used very carefully. If you choose to submerge the buckle in a cleaning solution, it is imperative that all areas of the buckle are blown dry when it is removed from the solution to reduce the possibility of corrosion or rust.

Brass, copper or silver that is tarnished can be cleaned with a metal polish. To restore brass, copper or silver to their original luster, you can use one of the available jewelry cleaners. CAUTION is again advised, most of the commercial cleaners will remove paint and the silver or gold backing on the rhinestones, or any shading. It is always best to start in an inconspicuous place. As your knowledge grows, you will be able to expand to a wider variety of methods.

Steel buttons or cut-steels can be brushed or wiped with a soft cloth. Lead from a lead pencil will remove light rust. An oil lubricant or any rust inhibiting solution, sprayed on a cloth, should then be applied. If the piece has pitted rust and you want to try and save it, use a fine steel wheel to remove the rust. It will most likely never look like new again but will be saved from the scrap bin.

Cleaning Metal Buckles

Before starting to clean a buckle it is best to examine it to make sure all stones are tight in their settings and other pieces are tight and in place. If the buckle is painted in any way, such as, shading, gold wash, enamels, lacquers or silver then caution must be exercised. Mild soap and water on a dampened cloth will remove most common dirt. Dry immediately with a soft dry cloth or towel. For more stubborn dirt a damp-

Cleaning Celluloid Buckles

Celluloid is easily cleaned with a damp cloth, but must be immediately wiped dry to prevent moisture from getting between the laminated layers which will cause the layers to separate. Metal trimmed celluloid should be cleaned with caution. Do not get water into the buckle as it will start to rust the metal from the inside out. Between the celluloid and the metal there is usually a cardboard backing that should remain dry.

Cleaning Enamel Buckles

Make sure your buckle is enameled and not painted before cleaning. Enamel is easily cleaned with a dampened cloth, and any metal can be polished with a metal polish. Be careful not to get metal polish on enamel, use a cotton swab if necessary to apply polish. Wipe dry or clean with a soft cloth. A light coat of hard wax can be applied to the enamel surface to enhance and protect it.

Cleaning Glass Buckles

Glass is easily cleaned with sudsy warm water or a diluted mixture of sudsy ammonia, or window or glass cleaner on a cloth. Glass with other decoration, rhinestones or metal should be cleaned with a damp cloth, and immediately dried.

Cleaning Pearl Buckles

The original shine can be returned by using mineral oil, or baby oil on a soft cloth. Do not clean this way when other decorations are on the piece. Clean with a soft cloth.

Cleaning Horn Buckles

Molded horn buckles with fine designs are generally full of dust and dirt. Light brushing and a fine coat of baby or mineral oil brightens them. Barton's Dyanshine shoe polish will restore the finish of black horn. Horn should be kept dry to prevent mildew.

Cleaning Ivory or Bone Buckles

If ivory or bone is yellow, cut a lemon in half, dip it in salt and rub over the surface. After drying, wipe with a damp cloth and buff dry.

Cleaning Ceramic Buckles

If the design is fired or fused into the ceramic, you may use warm sudsy water, a damp cloth or glass cleaner. If you suspect the design is not fired on the buckle, wipe carefully with a damp cloth. If in doubt about any part of the buckle, leave it alone.

Cleaning Wood Buckles

Brush out design or cracks with a brush, and buff with soft cloth. Use furniture polish or baby oil to clean a dirty buckle. Remember, anytime you put a liquid in wood , you risk the chance of changing the original color, forever.

Before cleaning quality buckles, it's always best to experiment with a damaged or unsalvageable piece to see what actually happens. After trying the selected method, set the piece aside for a week or so to see the final results. Minor buckle repairs should be restricted to those repairs that you are comfortable with, whereas more sophisticated repairs should be left to the professionals.

Glossary

Abalone. A mollusk having one shell. Pink, red, deep blue, and green shades are common colors of this iridescent shell.

Amber. The fossilized resin of extinct trees. Amber is light enough to float in water, and it is warm to the touch. Amber is usually yellowish, reddish, or brownish in color, though it can also be blue, green, orange, white or even black. It can be translucent or opaque and often is a mixture of the two.

Amethyst. A purple quartz gemstone that shows fiery twin colors of bluish purple and reddish purple.

Art Deco. A stilted, stylized design from 1910 to 1930, which was named after the 1925 L'Exposition Internationale des Arts Decoraftifs et Industriels Modernes, held in Paris, France. Art Deco was inspired by the art of the American Indian, ancient Egyptian, Greek, and Roman architecture.

Art Nouveau. A style of art, popular mainly from the 1890s and lasted till around 1910, characterized by flowing, curving, and interlacing lines. Dragonflies, vines, peacocks, flowers, dreamlike faces and figures, moons and moonlike stones, and metals were popular.

Aventurine. A kind of quartz spangled with bits of mica. Commonly referred to as goldstone.

Baguette. A gem, usually small, cut in the shape of a narrow rectangle.

Bakelite. A synthetic plastic invented in 1907 by Dr. Leo Hendrick Baekeland. The discovery of Bakelite is considered to have laid the foundation of the synthetic plastics industry. It is a combination of carbolic acid, formaldehyde, and lye.

Basse-Taille. A type of enameling in which a metal plate is cut to various depths into which translucent enamel is poured, achieving a three dimensional effect. The depth of the cut produces shadings from light to dark.

Berlin Iron. Berlin iron jewelry is jewelry made from case iron primarily at the Berlin Iron Foundry, though some cast iron jewelry was made in France in the late 1820s.

Bezel Setting. A metal rim or flange which holds a stone secure in its setting.

Black Glass. An imitation of jet.

Black Light. Invisible ultraviolet or infrared radiation. An ultraviolet lamp useful for identifying some materials. The light excites luminescence or fluorescence in some gemstones and nearly all natural materials.

Bohemian Garnet. Red or pyrope garnet, sometimes called Bohemian ruby. These were the favorite stones in inexpensive Bohemian jewelry.

Bone. This animal material was boiled, cleaned and cut to size in the making of buttons, buckles and other jewelry. Bone is often passed off as ivory, but bone and ivory are quite different in appearance. Bone is white or yellowish white, hard and dull in appearance unless it has been waxed or otherwise treated. If it is grained the grain is straight, brackish or grayish lines or dots. When it ages it yellows. Ivory is glossy and fat looking. It is creamy white, with brownish crosshatched graining, and as it ages it develops a distinctive beige patina.

Brass. An alloy of copper and zinc. To test brass, a drop of nitric acid will turn true brass green.

Cabochon. A stone cut in convex form, polished but not faceted. The back or base of the stone was usually left flat. Faceting did not appear until the Middle Ages. Cabochon stones were popular in the nineteenth century, and some stones are nearly always cabochon cut, like agates, turquoise, moonstones, cat's eye, and star gems of all kind.

Cameo. A stone or shell on which a design is carved in relief.

Carnelian. Red or reddish agate.

Casting. A process by which a model is reproduced by pouring a liquid casting material into a mold fashioned from the original. Characteristics of cast buckles include mold marks where the parts of the mold met and the material spread, air bubbles, texture and finish, and a lack of sharpness of definition.

Celluloid. A composition mainly of soluble guncotton and camphor which resembles ivory in texture and color. It was also dyed to imitate coral, tortoise shell, amber, and malachite. To test this material, apply a low degree of heat, and the celluloid will produce a carbolic acid odor. This odor can sometimes be induced by rubbing the surface until it is warm. A more definite test can be made by gently applying a hot needle.

Champleve Enamel. An enameling process in which areas of metal are cut, etched or routed and filled with enamel.

Channel Setting. A series of stones set together in a straight line with the sides of the mounting gripping the outer edges of the stones.

Cinnabar. This is the name given to the only important ore of mercury. One of its uses is as a pigment. Lacquer and other materials colored with cinnabar vary from a bright to a brownish red. The putty like material is built up on a base, then carved with fine tools.

Clasp. Two piece buckle, usually symmetrical in design.

Clip. Device used to hold, clamp or clasp something tightly or securely together. Clips can be ornamental and functional. Often referred to as dress or fur clips.

Cloisonné Enamel. A type of enameling in which thin wire made of silver, gold, bronze, or copper is guilded, then bent to form cells (cloisons). Each cell or cloison is then filled with enamel. Each color is in a separate compartment, each compartment separated by this thin wire.

Collet Setting. Another term for bezel. A round collar of metal that holds a gemstone in place.

Cut Steel. Cut steel was faceted and hand riveted to a buckle or a brooch frame. Cut and faceted steel beads were often used as spacers or decorative accents on cloth. Cut steel is often mistaken for marcasite.

Dealer. Person or persons who sell buttons and buckles at state and national functions.

Depose. A French word similar to United States "copyright" or "patent". The word is sometimes stamped on an article implying the article is meant for export or is imported.

Die Stamping. To cut a design into metal for mass production and reproduction.

Dress Clips. See clips.

Edwardian. Referring to the period of time encompassing the reign of England's King Edward VII, 1901-1910.

Electroplating. The process of covering metal with a coating of another metal by using electrical current.

Enamel. A glass like material used in powder or flux form and fired on to metal.

Engraving. A technique by which a design is put into a metal surface using incised lines.

Facet. Small flat surface cut into gemstones, rivets, glass, or shell. Its purpose is to refract light or enhance the design.

Facsimile. An exact copy.

Filigree. Ornamental designs made by using plain thread-like or plaited wire.

Fleur-de-lis. The term means "Flower of Light." The fleur-de-lis is the French symbol of life and power and is designed from nature's Iris. This symbol is found on jewelry from Edwardian to present time.

Foiling. Silver, gold or other thin leaf of metal used to back imitation gemstones or faceted glass to improve their color and provide greater brilliance.

Fracture. The characteristic way a stone breaks. Many stones can be identified by their fracture.

Garnet. A family of minerals that includes almandine garnet (purplish-red), demantoid (green), pyrope (blood red), spessaritite (brownish or yellowish red), and grossular (orange or brownish). Garnet is not dichroic (does not show two shades of color) and this helps in its identification. It does not fluoresce under black light, which distinguishes it from the ruby.

German Nickel or Silver. Metal which has no actual silver content but is an alloy of copper, zinc and nickel with the highest content being nickel which gives it a silvery white color. It is also called "French gray" or "gunmetal."

Gilt. A piece made of another metal very thinly covered with gold. In jewelry, silver gilt is silver beneath a thin coating of gold.

Girdle. The widest part of a faceted gemstone, the part that is gripped by the setting.

Gold. Precious metal ore containing alloys which vary depending on desired color and hardness.

Goldstone. Man made brown glass with specs of copper infused within, made as an imitation of Adventurine gemstone which contains particles of gold-colored minerals.

Gunmetal. An alloy of 90 percent copper and 10 percent tin that was very popular in the 1890s.

Gutta-Percha. A hard rubber material made from the sap of a Malayan tree. Discovered in the 1840s, it was used for making jewelry, statuary, and even furniture.

Hallmark. An official mark first adopted in England. The mark is incised, punched, or stamped on gold or silver to show quality and to signify purity of metal according to "sterling" or "caret" standard. Other countries' hallmarks indicate origin, patent and manufacturer.

Hat Buckle. Buckle used as adornment on a hat.

Horn and Hoof. These animal materials were ground up and mixed with other materials into a plastic composition. With a combination of moisture, heat, and pressure, the mixture was dyed and molded into various forms.

Inclusion. Foreign material such as gas, liquid, or mineral enclosed in a gemstone.

Inlay. To set one material into the body of another so that the surface is level.

Intaglio. An engraved stone in which the design is carved into the surface of the stone so that the rim is the highest portion. The opposite of a cameo.

Iridescent. To give a high luster to glass or other man made materials.

Ivory. The tusks of several animals, including elephant, hippopotamus, narwhal, walrus, and whale. Also includes vegetable ivory, which is made from the nut of the ivory palm tree. Elephant ivory is considered to be the true ivory.

Jade. A hard stone, usually green, with a resinous or oily aspect when polished. Jade is found in many shades and the presence of quantities of iron determine the color.

Japanned. A process developed as a substitute for expensive Oriental lacquering, about 1800, in England, France and Holland. The "synthetic lacquering" known as "Japanning" was simply a high grade of varnishing, with each coat being dried by heat before the next was applied.

Jet. A hard coal mined at Whitby, England, which was highly polished and carved. It was primarily sold as memorial jewelry.

Lalique, Rene. Famous French Art Nouveau designer.

Lapis Lazuli. Deep blue gemstone sometimes containing gold colored specks of iron pyrites.

Lava Jewelry. Lava found at Pompeii, Italy, which was primarily carved as cameos. It ranged in colors from cream to dark brown and white to charcoal. It is very soft and therefore permits a skilled artisan to carve fine detail with high relief.

Loupe. A jeweler's magnifying glass which is worn close to the eye. A 4x or 5x loupe is sufficient for most jewelry study.

Lucite. A trade name for clear plastic. It can be decorated in several ways.

Machine Stamping. A process by which a machine stamps designs into thin sheets of metal. Machine stamping was first used around the middle of the nineteenth century, but it was not until about 1870 that it took over. The great bulk of inexpensive jewelry was made this way.

Malachite. An opaque copper mineral marked with characteristic bright and darker bands of green.

Marcasite. A white iron pyrite. If the ore is yellow it takes on the appearance of "fools gold". Cut steel jewelry and marcasites resemble one another in color and faceted treatment, but cut steel rusts easily and is not as hard nor as brilliant as marcasites. Most marcasite jewelry is made in France.

Milk Glass. Oxide of tin added to the glass mix makes it opaque white. If there is a ting or tint in the original mix due to other oxides, the glass will not be pure white or milk white, but may be a faint green, blue, amber, or tan. But it will be opaque. Milk Glass was produced in Bristol, England in the mid- eighteen century and in the colonies and glass houses of the federal era. Milk Glass buckles are often painted in imitation of Chinese wares.

Millefiori. Multi-colored mosaic beads which requires great skill of the glassblower to create florals, animals, and intricate designs.

Mine Cut. Gems from South America, mostly Brazil, before diamonds were discovered in Africa. The cut differs from "European cut" in that it is thicker from the table to the cutlet (the bottom facet) and the point (or cutlet) is cut off flat. Some early glass for jewelry was cut with the rounded facets and duller finish and is referred to as *mine cut*.

Mosaic. Creating a motif or design parquetry with minute pieces of colored glass or stone which have been set into plaster. Individual portions of the design are sectioned by metal and are similar to the form used in cloisonné enameling.

Mother-of-pearl. The nacreous inner shell of mollusks that produce pearls. It has been used for jewelry and other decorative objects since Egyptian times.

Mourning Jewelry. Black jewelry, either real or imitation jet, black onyx, ebony, or bog oak.

Nickel Silver. Not silver, but an alloy of copper, nickel and zinc.

Obsidian. Natural volcanic glass that is usually black or gray in color.

Parure. A matching set of jewelry, usually containing three or more pieces of the following; necklace, choker, brooch, buckle, earrings, bracelet or ring.

Passementerie. Small separately molded pieces of glass not riveted but wired to a metal back and secured in place by bending the wires. The bits of glass may be dull or polished, or a combination of both. They were used as buckles and belt ornaments.

Paste. A superior glass containing oxide of lead used for jewelry to imitate gems and gemstones. Also known as *Strass*.

Pavé Setting. A style of setting stones where a number of stones are set as close together as possible.

Pavilion. The part of a cut gemstone that is below the girdle.

Pierce Work. Die cast frame which is cut and engraved with a great deal of open work in the metal.

Plastics. Term applied to group of synthetic chemical products with the distinct quality enabling them to be molded, carved, laminated or pressed into many shapes, sizes, and designs.

Polychrome Enamel. Enamel in various colors.

Porcelain. A fine white high-fired ceramic material sometimes used for portrait or picture paintings.

Pot Metal. Any alloy of scrap metals of various kinds.

Pressed Glass. Pressed glass is extremely common to buckles. The production of pressed glass requires the use of soft glass and heated molds. As a result of the pressing process, pressed glass lacks the brilliance of blown glass, but brilliant sparkle can be imparted by reheating or fire polishing after it has been pressed.

Prong Set. Method of attaching gemstones to a mount by use of four or more slender tines.

Rhinestone. Faceted glass set with a foil backing to give it highlights and brilliance. Also known as "brilliants."

Rub Over Setting. A closed setting in which the metal is worked up over the rim of the stone and evened out level with it.

Satsuma. A Japanese pottery or semiporcelain first made in the province of Satsuma, from which its name is derived.

Scalloped. Continuous series of rounded projections forming an edge, as in a pie crust.

Scarab. Form of a beetle that is the Egyptian symbol of longevity. After King Tut's tomb was opened in 1920, Egyptian motifs, the scarab in particular were widely used in jewelry.

Semiprecious Stone. An imprecise term, it generally means any gemstone other than sapphire, ruby, diamond, or emerald.

Shell Cameo. The helmet shell (brown and white) and the shell of the giant conch (pink and white) are the most commonly used types for cameo carving.

Shoe Buckle. Ornamented clasp or buckle for shoes.

Silver. The most common of precious metals. Fine silver is pure silver and is normally too soft to make jewelry. The alloy most often used is Sterling silver, which is 925 parts of silver to 75 parts copper.

Strass. See paste.

Synthetic. Produced artificially by chemical means, not real.

Trademark. The mark registered with the United States Patent Office that identifies a wholesaler or retailer.

Tortoise. Blonde, translucent amber or dark opaque reddish amber color of the Hawksbill and Loggerhead turtle shells. Can be molded, inlaid, and carved into jewelry.

Trembler. A short spring which causes an ornamental head to bobble or bounce freely. Sometimes used to accentuate a gemstone.

Trichot. A French manufacturer who devised a cheaper method of making a facsimile of cut steel, by stamping an openwork pattern into a single piece of steel.

Turquoise. A blue or blue-green gem mineral, soft and porous with a hardness of only 6.

Victorian. Referring to the time encompassing the reign of England's Queen Victoria, 1837-1901.

Bibliography

Albert, Lillian Smith, and Kathryn Kent. *The Complete Button Book* Garden City: Doubleday & Company, Inc., 1949.

Baker, Lillian. *100 Years of Collectible Jewelry*.: Collector Books, 1978.

Brown, Dorothy Foster. *Button Parade*. Chicago: Lightner Publishing Corp., 1942.

Couse, L.Erwina and Marguerite. *Button Classics*, Chicago, Lightner Publishing Co., 1941.

Epstein, Diana, and Millicent Safro. *Buttons*. New York: Harry N. Abrams, Inc., 1991.

Fink, Nancy. and Maryalice Ditzler. *Buttons*. Philadelphia Courage Books, 1993.

Hardy, R. Allen. *The Jewelry Repair Manual*. New York: Prentice Hall Press, 1986.

Hughes, Elizabeth, and Marion Lester. *The Big Book of Buttons*. Boyertown: Boyertown Publishing Company, 1981.

Henzel, S. Sylvia. *Collectible Costume Jewelry*. Lombard: Wallace-Homestead Book Company, 1987.

Jargstorf, Sibylle. *Baubles, Buttons and Beads*. Atglen: Schiffer Publishing Ltd., 1993.

Lester, Katherine Morris, and Bess Viola Oerke. *Accessories of Dress Peoria*: The Manual Arts Press, 1940.

Luscomb, Sally C. *The Collector's Encyclopedia of Buttons*. New York: Crown Publishers, Inc, 1967.

The National Button Society. *"Button Basics: How to Clean Buttons."* The National Button Bulletin. Vol. 52, No. 4 Oct 1993:222-227.

The National Button Society. *"Heartland Holi days."* The National Bulletin Society Bulletin. Vol. 55, No. 2 May 1996:86-91.

The National Button Society. *"Some Summer Cleaning Tips for Button Collectors."* The National Society Bulletin. Vol.54, No. 3 July 1995:159.

The National Button Society. *Official NBS Classification System*. February 1996 Edition.

Newman, Harold. *An Illustrated Dictionary of Jewelry*. London: Thames and Hudson Ltd., 1981.

Osborne, Peggy Ann. *About Buttons*. Atglen: Schiffer Publishing Ltd., 1994.

Peacock, Primrose. *Discovering Old Buttons*. Great Britain: Shire Publication Ltd., 1978.

Romero, Christie. *Warman's Jewelry*. Radnor: Wallace-Homestead Book Company. 1995.

Schiffer, Nancy. *Rhinestones!* Atglen: Schiffer Publishing, Ltd., 1993.

Index